SHE URGED MARY LOU TO EAT

A LITTLE MAID
OF
VIRGINIA

BY

ALICE TURNER CURTIS

AUTHOR OF
THE LITTLE MAID'S HISTORICAL SERIES
STORIES OF THE CIVIL WAR, ETC.

ILLUSTRATED BY
ELIZABETH PILSBRY

APPLEWOOD BOOKS
BEDFORD, MASSACHUSETTS

A Little Maid of Virginia was first published by the Penn
Publishing Company in 1922.

ISBN 1-55709-333-4

Thank you for purchasing an Applewood Book.
Applewood reprints America's lively classics—
books from the past that are still of interest to modern readers.
For a free copy of our current catalog, write to:
Applewood Books, Box 365, Bedford, MA 01730.

10 9 8 7 6 5 4 3 2

Printed and bound in Canada.

Library of Congress Cataloging-in-Publication Data
Curtis, Alice Turner.
    A little maid of Virginia / by Alice Turner Curtis, illustrated
by Elizabeth Pilsbry
        p.   cm.
    Summary: In the spring of 1781 at her home near Yorktown,
Virginia, eleven-year-old Rose Elinor Moore and her young
cousin share adventures, including witnessing the surrender of
Lord Cornwallis.
    ISBN 1-55709-333-4
    1. Virginia—History—Revolution, 1775–1783—Juvenile fic-
tion.   [1. Virginia—History—Revolution, 1775–1783—
Fiction.   2. United States—History—Revolution,
1775–1783—Fiction.]   I. Pilsbry, Elizabeth, ill.   II. Title.
PZ7.C941Lmvi   1998
[Fic]–dc21   97-53240
                                            CIP
                                            AC

Introduction

ROSE ELINOR MOORE was eleven years old when her little cousin, Mary Lou Abbott, came to live with her at the beautiful home of her parents near Yorktown. This was in the spring of 1781 during the War of the Revolution. The two little girls had many exciting adventures and witnessed a great deal of the action which took place there. They even met and talked to the Marquis de Lafayette. In the fall of 1781 Rose Elinor and Mary Lou with Mr. and Mrs. Moore drove to Yorktown to witness Cornwallis's surrender. There they saw Washington, Lafayette, Rochambeau, Von Steuben and Knox awaiting the arrival of the British generals. These are only a few of the interesting things which occur in *A Little Maid of Virginia*.

Contents

Illustrations

A LITTLE MAID OF VIRGINIA

CHAPTER I

ROSECREST

ROSE ELINOR MOORE had just passed her eleventh year when her little cousin, Mary Lou Abbott, came from a town beyond the Blue Ridge, in the Valley of Virginia, to live with the Moores at Rosecrest, their beautiful home on the York River.

The house was built on a hill not far from the river; and its fine gardens with tall cedar trees, and box-lined paths, had roses of many colors whose fragrance drifted in through the open doors and windows of the house. Rose-bushes climbed up the porch and around the windows; delicate yellow roses, that first blossomed with Virginia's April butter-cups; beautiful white Yorks; rich damask roses, and sweet hundred-leafs. Rose Elinor often wondered if she had been named "Rose" on account of the garden, or if the place had been named "Rosecrest" because her own name was Rose. She liked to think that the place had really been named for her; but she had never asked, half-afraid that she would discover that she had been called Rose because of the beautiful garden.

From the top of the house, where there was a broad flat space, over which was stretched a canvas awning, one could look up and down the broad York River for miles and miles, and here in the early evenings Mr. Moore and his visitors often sat, watching the white-sailed ships passing up the broad stream or down to the sea.

Rose thought this the most pleasant part of the big house. She had her own chair and footstool there, and a square wooden box in which to keep her playthings, and her work-basket; and she was sitting there one May afternoon when her mother told her about little Mary Lou Abbott, whose own mother was dead, and whose father was a soldier in Washington's army, for it was the spring of 1781, when British forces under Lord Cornwallis were advancing into Virginia.

Rose knew that Mary Lou was two years younger than herself, that her eyes were blue and her hair yellow. She knew that since Mary Lou was two years old she had not had a home of her own, but had lived first in the home of one relative and then in the home of another. "But now," said Mrs. Moore, "she is to stay with us, unless the British take Yorktown and destroy Rosecrest; and you must treat her as if she were your younger sister."

"Is she to live here always?" asked Rose, her face clouding.

"This is to be her home, just as it is yours, Rose," said Mrs. Moore; "and now I must go down-stairs and tell Mammy Zella that after today she will have two little girls instead of one to take care of."

"Is she to have my mammy, too?" exclaimed Rose, jumping up from her seat; but her mother had already vanished down the twisting staircase which led from the roof to the upper hall and did not hear the question; and if she had looked back and had seen Rose stamp her little slippered foot and shake her head so fiercely that her black curls danced wildly about her flushed face, she would indeed have thought that some wicked fairy had taken possession of her small daughter.

"I don't want her! I don't want her!" Rose whispered angrily. "Father and Mother and Mammy will all like her just as much as they do me; and Mother says that I must share everything I have with her, because Mary Lou hasn't any home. But she could stay with Aunt Pamela, who hasn't any children and is an old maid. That's where Mary Lou ought to stay," and after a moment she whispered softly: "If Mary Lou Abbott was a Tory, if she wanted England to conquer America, I know Father would send her straight back to Aunt Pamela! I'm sure he would. And even if Aunt Pamela is poor and old, I guess she could take care of one little girl. Perhaps I'll find out that Mary Lou Abbott is a Tory, after all," and now Rose was smiling happily. As she opened the wooden box and took out the work-bag of blue-and-silver striped silk, that her mother had given her on her eleventh birthday, she began to think of some way in which she could convince her father that the little cousin, who would reach Rosecrest the next day, was disloyal to the American cause.

All the household at Rosecrest did their best to spoil the little girl, and her quick temper and selfishness were passed over as trivial faults. So it was not to be wondered at that Rose Elinor resented sharing her home with a cousin whom she had never seen.

It was late the next afternoon when one of the queerest vehicles that had ever entered the fine drive-way which led to the main entrance of Rosecrest came slowly up the hill. An ancient gray donkey, whose harness had been mended with strings, draw-ing a two-wheeled wagon that was shaped like a box, and in which was seated a small girl, whose yellow head was just visible above the top of the sides of the wagon. An old negro, perched on a chair that was evi-dently nailed to the front of the wagon, was urging the mule on, calling out: "Gee dup, Solomon! Ain' yo' old 'nuff yit to un'stan' wot I tells ye?" and he would then bring down the slender switch lightly on Solomon's tough hide.

"It's old Pete!" exclaimed Mr. Moore. "What was Aunt Pamela thinking of to let him drive little Mary Lou in that wagon," and as he spoke Mr. Moore ran down the drive and the old mule came to a full stop, and stood with drooping head as its driver stepped down from his seat, and saluted the master of Rosecrest:

"Yas, sah! Thar' we is, Miss Mary Lou an' me, Massa Moore. We's rid de twenty-five mile since daybreak," and the old darkey looked reproachfully at Solomon as he added: "Dat mule is sho' too lazy to trabbel."

Mr. Moore looked anxiously at the little girl in the wagon. "You must be very tired, my dear," he said kindly, "but perhaps you would rather walk up the driveway than ride any farther in that uncomfortable carriage. I am your father's cousin, and am glad to welcome you to Rosecrest."

The little girl stood up and Mr. Moore lifted her over the side of the wagon, and noticed that she was taller than Rose, and that she looked a little frightened and unhappy.

"Your Cousin Rose is waiting to see you," he said, smiling down at the little girl whose face was nearly hidden from sight by a sunbonnet of checked blue gingham, and whose queerly-shaped blue cotton dress hung straight from her shoulders. As Mr. Moore looked at his small visitor his eyes softened.

"Poor child," he thought, pitifully, remembering how Mary Lou had never known the care and affection of a mother, and that she had been an unwelcome member of the household of her Great-aunt Pamela Cutting; and he resolved that henceforth Mary Lou should be treated with the same affection that was lavished on his own little daughter.

Uncle Pete and "Solomon" had vanished down the road to the stables, where they were warmly welcomed,—and where "Solomon" promptly decided to remain for life, before Mary Lou and Mr. Moore reached the wide porch where Mrs. Moore and Rose were waiting. Rose wore one of her prettiest dresses. It was of pale pink muslin, with tiny white embroidered rosebuds, and a sash of soft white silk. Her stockings were of the finest white cotton, and her ankle-ties of patent leather. A broad ribbon of pink held her dark curls in place, and as she stood looking down at the forlorn little figure that came stumbling up the steps it was no wonder that Mary Lou's eyes filled with admiring surprise, and that she thought her Cousin Rose the most beautiful creature that she had ever beheld.

Rose's face softened at Mary Lou's look of adoring admiration. After all, she thought, perhaps this new cousin might prove just one more person who would do all she could to make Rose Elinor Moore happy. For the moment she decided to give Mary Lou a chance to remain at Rosecrest; the newcomer was so shabby and forlorn that even Rose Elinor's selfish plans toward her were for the moment forgotten; and as her glance met Mary Lou's she put out both her hands and clasped her cousin's thin little fingers.

As the two girls stood hand in hand Mr. and Mrs.

Moore smiled at each other in delight. They felt sure
that the cousins would be friends, and that their own
little daughter would be happier through having Mary
Lou as a companion.

"Oh! Where is my box!" Mary Lou exclaimed suddenly, drawing her hands from her cousin's, and looking about with anxious eyes.

"Where did Uncle Pete go? My other dress is in the
box, and all my things!" she continued, evidently ready
to cry at the thought of their possible loss.

"Your box is safe, dear. It will be in your room," Mrs.
Moore assured her. "And remember that now you are
our little girl, and that we mean you to be very happy
at Rosecrest."

A little flush crept over the thin little face, and Rose
came a little nearer and whispered: "Mary Lou, aren't
you hungry?"

"Yes," responded Mary Lou nodding vigorously. "I
haven't had anything to eat since morning. Uncle Pete
lost our lunch-basket."

"There! I knew she was hungry!" declared Rose Elinor, and seizing her cousin's hand she drew her into the
big hall and toward the dining-room calling: "Mammy
Zella! Mammy Zella! Clippy! Clippy!" and instantly
Clippy, a stout negro girl, appeared, quickly followed
by Mammy Zella, and both the negro women hurried
off to carry out their young mistress's demand that
food: "Cakes and milk and bread and honey, and chick-

en and everything," should at once be brought to the dining-room for Mary Lou.

It was Rose who untied the strings of the ugly sun-bonnet and smoothed back Mary Lou's straggling locks, who drew a chair close to a round table near the long, open window that overlooked the garden and nearly pushed her cousin into it; and then stood close beside her when Clippy and Mammy Zella brought the food, and urged Mary Lou to eat.

CHAPTER II

GREAT-AUNT PAMELA

MISS PAMELA FAIRFAX CUTTING was a sister to the mother of Mr. Stephen Moore, and the great-aunt of Rose Elinor and Mary Lou. She lived with a few faithful servants in a shabby old house about twenty-five miles distant from Yorktown; and since the beginning of the Revolutionary War she had kept closely at home. When her nephew Fairfax Abbott had joined Washington's army she had refused to ever see him again; but she had taken his motherless little daughter, Mary Lou, into her home, and when she declared that she would make "a real Tory" out of her little great-niece, none of her loyal American relatives paid any attention to what they called "Aunt Pamela's silly talk." But Miss Pamela Cutting meant exactly what she said.

Mary Lou's first lessons were the names and deeds of England's kings and queens. She was told the story of brave Sir Walter Raleigh, and that it was he who had named the colony Virginia; and Great-aunt Pamela impressed upon her little niece that all England's laws for governing her American Colonies were just and right; and not until Mary Lou went to Roscrest did she ever hear the real cause of the conflict between England and America. In fact, Mary Lou was a little Tory; just as Rose Elinor, before her cousin arrived at Rosecrest, had hoped, in order that she might prove unwelcome and be sent back to Great-aunt Pamela.

Great-aunt Pamela had lived alone for so many years that she knew but little of how other people carried on their lives. She thought that little girls should always be quiet; that they should be content to sit quietly indoors and learn difficult lessons, and be very proud to sew neatly, to knit, and to help with the lighter household tasks, so that when they grew up they would be accomplished housekeepers.

She thought it was wicked to buy ribbons and sashes and muslin dresses for a little girl; and, although she did not mean to be harsh, she was constantly reproving Mary Lou for the way she spoke, walked, entered a room, or made a curtsey; so that when Mary Lou came to Rosecrest to live she was shy, awkward, and afraid to speak.

Her father had written to Mr. Moore asking him to give his little daughter a home, and had also written Aunt Pamela that Mary Lou was to be sent to Rosecrest, for he did not want her to remain in a Tory household; and while Great-aunt Pamela declared it was the best news she had received for many a day, she nevertheless felt it very unfair and cruel that she must give up the little girl. Mary Lou had wept bitterly at the thought of going to a new home. Before she had lived with Great-aunt Pamela she had lived with relatives of her mother's, where she had been unkindly treated, and it seemed to her that there was no place in all the world for a motherless child whose father was an American soldier, and she feared to go to a new place.

But her welcome to Rosecrest had been like entering a new world, and when she opened her eyes on the morning after her arrival her first thought was of her beautiful Cousin Rose Elinor. She looked about the big pleasant chamber, half fearful that she had been dreaming and might find herself in the tiny, closet-like room at Great-aunt Pamela's, and gave a sigh of content as she realized that the roses nodding in at the open window were real roses; their delicate fragrance filled the air, and Mary Lou recalled the beautiful garden through which the old mule "Solomon" had dragged her clumsy wagon on the previous afternoon, and again she sighed with content that her journey had ended so happily.

As she lay smiling at the thought of the warm welcome she had received, the chamber door was gently pushed open and Rose Elinor stood in the doorway looking anxiously toward the bed where Mary Lou lay, and as she noticed her cousin's welcoming smile Rose Elinor's own face beamed with delight. But she did not speak, and as she advanced into the room Mary Lou saw that Rose Elinor's arms were full, and she sat quickly up in bed and watched her wonderingly.

Rose Elinor approached a big cushioned chair and very carefully lowered her burden into it; then she turned toward the bed and nodded triumphantly.

"For you, Mary Lou! All my white clothes, and stockings and shoes. Jump up and try them on, and if my things do not fit you Clippy or Mammy shall take us to Yorktown and see if we cannot buy things there for you."

In a moment Mary Lou was out of bed and, gazing at Rose Elinor with adoring eyes, she exclaimed: "You are like a fairy, or an angel, who brings good gifts. You look like an angel, but you are a real girl, aren't you?" and her eyes had such a pleading look, her voice was so serious, and she seemed so pitiful and alone, that again Rose Elinor's heart was touched, and she put her arm about her cousin and kissed her thin cheek.

"Of course I'm real. I'm Rose Elinor, and I am going to give you everything you want, everything!" she declared earnestly, and when an hour later Mammy entered the room she held up both hands in surprise, for Rose Elinor had tugged the oval tin bathing tub in from her own room, had called Clippy to fill it with warm water, and had helped bathe Mary Lou, and was now vigorously brushing her cousin's hair; while Clippy, with open mouth and rolling eyes, was vainly endeavoring to pull on to Mary Lou's feet a pair of white open-worked cotton stockings.

It was quickly discovered that Rose Elinor's clothing would not fit her cousin, but Mammy promptly announced that seams could be let out, and tucks taken, so that Mary Lou could wear Rose Elinor's dresses and skirts until new ones could be made for her, but the shoes and stockings were too small; so although Mary Lou came down to breakfast smiling with delight in a ruffled muslin dress, her well-brushed yellow hair tied with a pink ribbon such as she had never dared even to hope to possess, she was obliged to wear her own clumsily made shoes and coarse knit blue stockings.

"Clippy can take us to Yorktown right away after breakfast," Rose Elinor announced, as she heaped spoonfuls of honey on Mary Lou's plate. "You know, Mother, that the storekeeper has rows of slippers for little girls, and Mammy must manage to have stockings ready for her."

Mrs. Moore agreed to the plan, well pleased to see Rose Elinor so happily occupied, and thinking that her little daughter had the warmest heart in the world to be so anxious to bestow gifts on the cousin whom she had never before seen.

Rose Elinor could hardly spare time to eat her own breakfast, she was so eager to make sure that Mary Lou had the best of everything; and even the servants wondered what had come over their young mistress, for Rose Elinor was usually whining out demands for some dainty, or finding fault because her breakfast was not more quickly served. But now all her attention was fixed on her cousin, and she was quick to notice how straight Mary Lou held herself, and how daintily she clasped her fork and used her spoon. Great-aunt Pamela had been very stern with the little girl in regard to these things. "Ladies do not loll on the table, or make a noise with their knives, or ask to be served," she had constantly reminded her niece, and Mary Lou's table manners were perfect.

"Rose Elinor seems to have taken full charge of her cousin," said Mr. Moore smilingly, as Rose clasped Mary Lou's hand and led her from the dining-room.

"Indeed she has; she just informed me that Mary Lou must have two pairs of kid slippers, two hats, and a pink muslin exactly like her own," responded Mrs. Moore, with evident satisfaction. "And Mary Lou seems to think that whatever Rose Elinor says settles every question."

"Well, it is fortunate for both of them that Rose Elinor is pleased. I hope poor little Mary Lou did not hear too much of Aunt Pamela's disloyal talk. It would indeed be a pity if the child has been taught to become a traitor to the cause of America's freedom, for which her own father is fighting," said Mr. Moore gravely.

But Mrs. Moore declared that Mary Lou was too young to understand the meaning of the word "Tory." She did not know that Aunt Pamela had convinced the little girl that "Tory" meant a brave and loyal person who defended England's acts, and that Mary Lou would be proud indeed to be called by that name.

The week of Mary Lou's arrival at Rosecrest was the very week when Lord Cornwallis and his troops arrived at Petersburg, Virginia, determined to conquer the state. Mr. Moore had heard this news with grave fears; he was himself an American soldier, but had not yet recovered from wounds received when Savannah was captured by the English in 1778, and now could only serve the American cause by giving liberally, and by the earnestness and frequency of his efforts to uphold the justice of his country's right to govern itself, and Rose Elinor had been quite right when she had told herself that not even a little girl who was a Tory would be a welcome guest at Rosecrest.

But while Mr. Moore's thoughts were sadly troubled over Lord Cornwallis's arrival on Virginia's soil, Rose Elinor and Mary Lou were happily driving off toward Yorktown, with Clippy on the front seat of the wagon beside the Moores' trusted coachman, Black Jasper, who often drove Rose Elinor and Clippy about the pleasant country roads.

Rose Elinor sat close beside Mary Lou and now and then looked a little anxiously at her cousin, as if to make sure that Mary Lou was enjoying the drive. It was perhaps the first time in all her life that Rose Elinor had thought of the happiness of another person before her own.

The road led through cultivated fields and woods of lofty pines, hollies, laurels and tall oak-trees; now and then there were glimpses of York River, and very soon they reached the main street of the village of Yorktown, that was built on high ground on the south bank of the river. They drove past the "Swan" Tavern, and Rose Elinor called to the coachman to stop at "Mr. Mason's store," and Jasper, with a fine flourish of his whip, brought his horses to a standstill directly in front of a long, one-storied building in whose windows were displayed a variety of articles, at which Mary Lou gazed with admiring eyes.

"Oh! Rose Elinor! There are shoes and slippers, and there is a doll, and see the fine tin pans and the blue pitcher!" she exclaimed as Clippy helped her to descend from the high wagon, and the two little girls entered the shop.

"There are not many things, Mary Lou," Rose Elinor responded, "but we can surely get you some shoes," and the two cousins entered the shop.

The storekeeper had no trouble in fitting Mary Lou to a pair of fine kid slippers with tiny silver buckles and to a pair of ankle-ties whose straps buttoned about her ankles, just as did those worn by Rose Elinor. Then the two little girls wandered about the long, narrow shop looking at the various things that were for sale, while Mr. Mason, the old storekeeper, explained that it was now very difficult to get anything.

"The British have shut off our supplies for so long that I have only my old stock, but their day is nearly over and very soon American ships will sail the seas in safety and bring us all we lack," he said, smiling down at the little girls.

"My father says there are no Tories in Virginia, and that Lord Cornwallis will be driven into the sea," declared Rose Elinor, at the same time pointing to a doll that stood in the corner of the window and added: "I think my little cousin would like that doll."

Mary Lou fairly gasped with delight as the old storekeeper smilingly handed her the doll. It was not a very beautiful doll, and its muslin dress was rather faded and dingy, for it had stood in the window for many weeks, but to Mary Lou, who had never possessed a doll, it seemed lovely beyond words and she clasped it eagerly.

"Mammy will make suitable clothes for it," said Rose Elinor carelessly.

"Oh, Cousin Rose Elinor, I will make things for it, all its things," declared Mary Lou earnestly; "and may I not hold it until we get home? You see, I never held a doll before!"

"Never held a doll!" exclaimed Rose Elinor. "Well, I do think Great-aunt Pamela is a hateful, stingy old Tory not to have given you a doll. And to think I have four! And you shall have them all, Mary Lou; for of course now that I am eleven years old and nearly a young lady, I do not want to play with dolls. You shall have them this very afternoon."

While the two little girls were talking about dolls the old storekeeper had been searching about the shelves and now came toward them carrying a small, square brass box. He set it down on the counter and lifted the cover, and Rose Elinor, as well as Mary Lou, exclaimed in delighted admiration: "Beads!" For the box was divided into compartments, and each of these was filled with shining beads. There were white beads of such crystal clearness that they resembled heaped-up dew-drops; there were beads of so vivid a green that they looked like bits of young birch leaves after a rain, and blue beads of every shade from the pale color of forget-me-nots to the deep blue of spring-time skies. There were beads as golden as sunlight, pale pink and deep red beads; in fact, there was hardly a color or a shape in which beads are made that the brass box did not contain.

"Perhaps you may like to make necklaces for your dolls," said the storekeeper smilingly.

"It is a fine present, Mr. Mason, and my cousin and I thank you very kindly," Rose Elinor said, and Mary Lou repeated the words after her, quite sure that whatever Rose Elinor said was the best possible way of expressing appreciation.

The two little girls started for home well pleased with their morning's excursion. Mary Lou held the doll closely in her arms and the package containing her new Slippers rested beside her, while Rose Elinor held the box of beads.

"We will begin to string necklaces this very afternoon," said Rose Elinor. "Oh, Mary Lou, before you came I hoped that you might turn out a Tory!" she added suddenly, looking kindly at her sober-faced little cousin, and feeling ashamed that she had even wished that Mary Lou should not stay at Rosecrest.

Mary Lou's blue eyes shone happily and she smiled radiantly at her cousin, quite sure that what she was about to say would make Rose Elinor even more pleased with her.

"Of course I am a Tory, Cousin Rose Elinor. I am loyal to the sacred cause of England and King George," she declared in the very words Great-aunt Pamela Fairfax Cutting had taught her.

CHAPTER III

A YOUNG TORY

"OH, Mary Lou!" Rose's voice was nearly a wail, and Clippy turned quickly in her seat to see what was the trouble with her young mistress, but before she could speak Rose Elinor exclaimed: "I nearly dropped the box of beads," as indeed she had, in her horror and surprise at Mary Lou's declaration that she was a Tory.

Clippy muttered to herself that "I knowed dat chile wouldn't get home 'thout wailin' 'bout som't'ing," for Rose's unexpected good-nature since her cousin's arrival had surprised all the servants, and Clippy had confided to Mammy Zella that such behavior was too good to last.

But Clippy's anxious look had added to Rose Elinor's trouble over her cousin's words, for she had instantly resolved that no one must discover that Mary Lou was a traitor to America's cause. It would not do for anyone belonging to Rosecrest to hear the little girl declare herself a Tory.

"It's all Great-aunt Pamela's fault," said Rose Elinor, and Mary Lou looked at her wonderingly.

28

"I suppose you mean my not having a doll," she responded questioningly, "but Great-aunt Pamela thought only of what was good for me; she used to say so every day."

"Well, I despise her!" said Rose Elinor wrathfully, and her black eyes seemed to snap with anger, and Mary Lou's thin little face again grew anxious and sorrowful.

They were now passing through a grove of tall locust-trees whose blossoms filled the air with fragrance; a mocking-bird was singing as if to declare the world was a joyful place to visit, and for a moment Rose Elinor forgot Great-aunt Pamela's faults and Mary Lou's dangerous words and exclaimed, "This is the prettiest place on Yorktown highway. Stop the horses, Jasper," she called, "I want to show Mary Lou the old mill."

Jasper promptly obeyed; and Clippy, a little sulky at the delay, helped the two little girls from the wagon.

"It's too pleasant to go straight home," said Rose Elinor, taking her cousin's hand, "and I heard Father say he would not want Jasper this morning, so we can walk about here, and you can tell me more about hateful old Great-aunt Pamela."

Mary Lou stood still and a half-frightened look came into her blue eyes. Already she loved Rose Elinor better than anyone except the soldier-father whom she so seldom saw; to have this lovely cousin who was so unbelievably kind to her, think her ungrateful made poor little Mary Lou's heart beat uncomfortably; but

Great-aunt Pamela, in spite of her stern ways, had never been really unkind to her little niece; in fact, compared with her previous abiding place, Great-aunt Pamela's home seemed a pleasant place to Mary Lou, and her loyal soul demanded that she should defend an absent friend, but it took all her courage to say:

"Please, dear Rose Elinor, Great-aunt Pamela is not hateful, and she was always telling me my faults and trying to make me a better girl, and teach me to grow up loyal to England and England's cause."

Rose Elinor snatched her hand from Mary Lou's clasping fingers and stamped her slippered foot angrily.

"Stop! Stop!" she screamed. "Don't you dare, never as long as you live, to say that again. And your own father a loyal American soldier. England's king is America's enemy. If my father knew you were a Tory he would send you straight back to Great-aunt Pamela!" And Rose instantly forgot her desire to shield her cousin and keep anyone from discovering that she was a Tory.

Mary Lou held her doll more tightly than ever; tears gathered in her blue eyes as she responded in a faltering voice: "But you said that you hoped I was a Tory, Rose Elinor. You said you hoped—" but she could say no more and turning away from her cousin she ran stumbling along the path that led toward the old mill, on Wormeley Creek.

When Mary Lou began speaking Rose Elinor had quickly turned her back on her cousin and ran along the woodland road over which they came; therefore, she did not know that Mary Lou was running in the opposite direction, but believed her standing near the tall oak-tree where they had halted, and in a moment she found herself near the highway, where the bay horses were moving uneasily and where Black Jasper and Clippy were complaining to each other over the selfishness of their young mistress in keeping them waiting in so lonely a spot.

But as Rose Elinor found herself near the wagon she realized that she must not let Clippy discover that she had left her cousin alone in the woods, and, before either Clippy or Jasper had seen her, she turned quickly into a wayside path. She did not start back at once, but sat down on an old moss-covered log.

"I wish Mary Lou had stayed at Great-aunt Pamela's," she thought bitterly, quite forgetting all her plans for the humble little cousin, for whom she had instantly felt so sorry, and whose adoring looks had promptly won Rose Elinor's approval. It was not long before she heard Clippy's voice calling: "Miss Rose Elinor! Miss R-o-s-e El-i-*nor*!" but the little girl made no response.

"She can call and call, if she wants to. I suppose the little Tory is back at the wagon and wants to go to Rose-crest, but they can all wait until I am ready to go. They won't dare start without me," thought the angry girl, leaning back against a big hickory-tree, whose branches drooped nearly to the ground.

After a time the calls ceased and soon Rose Elinor heard the breaking of twigs and the movement of branches, and then again her own name called in anxious tones, and realized that Clippy had come in search of her.

"She shan't find me," thought Rose Elinor, and was instantly on her feet looking about for a hiding-place. To crouch behind the log might serve, but Rose Elinor felt sure that Clippy would be quick to discover such a hiding place. A low-hanging bough of the big hickory was just above her head; reaching up Rose clasped it with both hands, and was able to draw herself up and scramble to a seat close to the trunk of the tree, where the small branches and thickly growing leaves hid her from sight, and she was not a moment too soon; the big branch was still moving and rustling when Clippy came down the path and stopped directly beneath the tree to call in frightened tones: "Ro-s-e *El*inor!" adding, "I dunno w'at I'll do if I can't fin' dat chile."

Rose nearly lost her balance in trying to get a good look at Clippy. For the moment the little girl had entirely forgotten her Tory cousin in the fun of hiding away from the anxious Clippy, and when Clippy exclaimed: "Like as not dar's a panther a-crouchin' in dat hickory-tree all ready to spring right down an' eat me," it was all Rose could do to keep from laughing outright. In a moment, however, Clippy started on, her calls growing fainter and fainter until they could no longer be heard.

"Somet'ing's got dose chillun!" Clippy informed Jasper on her return to where the coachman anxiously awaited her. "If Rose Eli-*nor* was by herse'f I'd say her misch'ef was at de bottom ob it! But she ain' by herse'f. Dat solemn liddle cousin ain' gwine to hide up fum us. So dar's some animal got 'em."

But Black Jasper shook his head at this statement: "If 'twas an animile we'd heered screeches," he responded soberly, "but it's mighty plain dat trubble has befall dem lille gals. An' wot yo' t'inks gwine to happen to us, Clippy, w'en we 'rives at Rosecres' widout 'em?"

"Oh, my lan', Jasper!" wailed Clippy. "I mos' wish a panther had ketched me."

Jasper promptly decided that all they could do now was to drive to Rosecrest as quickly as possible and tell exactly what had happened.

"Massa Moore, he'll know jes' w'at to do," said Jasper, as he started the bay horses off at their best pace, and with Clippy beside him wailing and sobbing over the missing girls and her own probable punishment for permitting them out of her sight, they turned toward home.

For a time Rose Elinor kept as quiet as possible on her leafy perch, but it was not a comfortable resting place, and when she felt quite sure that Clippy had given up the search she again crawled along the big bough and lowered herself to the ground. She had lost her hair ribbon in the scramble among the branches, and torn her muslin dress in several places, but this did not trouble her; she had plenty of dresses at home, and Rose Elinor was never questioned or blamed for lost hair ribbons or torn gowns. She followed the path back to the highway, sure that she would find Black Jasper and Clippy and Mary Lou all awaiting her return.

As she stepped out into the road and found herself alone with no trace of the wagon or of Mary Lou, Jasper or Clippy, she was sure that she had mistaken the place; but as she looked about she saw where the horses had pawed the soft turf, and the marks of the wheels where the wagon had started off.

"They have gone and left me! Left me!" she exclaimed, hardly able to believe that such a thing could be possible. For a moment she stood looking forlornly up and down the deserted road; tears gathered in her eyes, and for the first time in her eleven years Rose Elinor found herself obliged to depend on herself.

"I'll have to walk home," she thought unhappily. "That mean old Clippy to let Jasper drive that Tory girl home and make me walk. I'll tell my father that she's a Tory the minute I get home," and the angry little girl started reluctantly on her long walk. She did not for a moment question but that Mary Lou was seated in the wagon riding toward Rosecrest.

Mary Lou had run blindly on until her foot caught in a trailing vine and she stumbled and fell, the treasured doll flying from her clasp into the underbrush. She was up in a second and, although her hands and knees were bruised, she did not stop to think of her hurts, but began a wild search after her doll, which to herself she had named "Lovely." She pushed into the tangle of laurel, looking about with woebegone sobs as she failed to discover "Lovely," but at last her search was rewarded, and she found her doll resting securely on the top of a thick growth of laurel, none the worse for the flight through the air.

CHAPTER IV

LOST IN THE RAVINE

THE May sunshine grew into noontime heat as Rose Elinor plodded along the dusty road toward Rosecrest. Her thin slippers were not suited for a long walk over the rough highway, and in a short time her feet ached so that every step hurt; nevertheless she walked resolutely forward. But the tears gathered in her eyes and rolled over her flushed cheeks and she gave vent to little angry sobs and exclamations of wrath toward Clippy, Jasper, Mary Lou and even Great-aunt Pamela, as she trudged wearily along.

Rose Elinor could hardly believe it possible that so dreadful a thing as to be left alone and apparently forgotten could really happen to Rose Elinor Moore of Rosecrest. "And all because that hateful Mary Lou is a Tory," she whimpered, as the road left the shade of the tall trees and led for a short distance above the river.

She had stopped for a moment's rest when she heard the clatter of horses' feet approaching, and instantly Rose Elinor's thoughts centered on her torn skirt and her untidy hair, and she realized that her face and hands were grimy with dust and that her white stockings were now more nearly gray than white. That any-one should discover her in such a plight was more than she could bear.

"It may be a riding party from Spottswood Man-sion, and they would indeed laugh to see such a fig-ure," she thought, and fled from the road to crouch behind the thick underbrush on the river's bank, where she could not be seen from the highway and where she could not get a glimpse of the party that rushed past at such a rapid pace that clouds of dust settled down upon her. Not for a moment did Rose Elinor imagine that it was her father who rode by, accompanied by a number of servants, with Jasper to show them the exact point where Rose Elinor and Mary Lou had entered the woodland path.

After returning to the road Rose Elinor decided to cross the fields as the shorter way to reach Rosecrest, and when she finally came into a path leading directly to the house there was no one about to notice her arrival, and she entered the wide hall and very slowly climbed the stairs to her chamber and with a sigh of utter exhaus-tion she sank down upon her bed, too tired to even call for Mammy Zella or reproach Clippy; and there, an hour later, Mrs. Moore discovered her little daughter sound asleep; and, taking it for granted that Mary Lou must have returned with Rose Elinor, a messenger was sent post-haste after the searching party to inform Mr. Moore that the little girls were safe at Rosecrest.

"Do not disturb Rose Elinor or her cousin," Mrs. Moore cautioned the servants, and no one even looked into Mary Lou's chamber, and not until the late afternoon when Rose Elinor awoke and with loud calls for "Mammy Zella! Clippy! Mammy Zella!" brought the entire household running to do her bidding, was it discovered that Mary Lou had not returned with her cousin to Rosecrest, and that Rose Elinor knew nothing of what had become of her.

"I think she has gone back to Great-aunt Pamela Fairfax Cutting," Rose Elinor declared, when Clippy told her that Mary Lou had not returned. But she said nothing about Mary Lou's announcement of being a Tory. If Mary Lou only would go back to Great-aunt Pamela and stay there, thought Rose Elinor, she would keep her cousin's traitorous declaration a profound secret.

"But the child could never walk such a distance. And how could she find the way? We must start Jasper after her at once," declared Mrs. Moore anxiously. "But why did she even think of such a thing as returning to Aunt Pamela? You made her so welcome, Rose, and she seemed so happy with you," she added thoughtfully.

Rose Elinor made no reply. She really believed that Mary Lou must have resented her words, and that she had at once started back to the only refuge she knew.

"I don't want her to come back, Mother," she announced, after a moment's silence.

But Mrs. Moore was just leaving the room and did not hear her. Mr. Moore decided that he would go himself to bring Mary Lou back to Rosecrest. He did not understand what could have happened so suddenly between Rose Elinor and her cousin to make Mary Lou start off in such a fashion, and he resolved to question his little daughter on his return.

It was now several hours since Black Jasper had driven home with the news of the disappearance of the cousins, and if Mary Lou had followed the highway over which she had driven with Uncle Pete on the previous day, she must now be miles away, but, mounted on a swift horse, Mr. Moore felt sure that he could overtake her in a short time, and started off hoping to bring her safely to Rosecrest before sundown.

As he rode along Mr. Moore kept a sharp outlook for some sign of the missing girl, hoping that she might have stopped to rest by the roadside; but the hours went by and when he rode up the drive to Aunt Pamela's weather-beaten old house it was late in the afternoon, and he was now almost sure that Mary Lou must have wandered from the highway and lost herself in the woodland paths.

Aunt Pamela listened to his quickly told story of Mary Lou's disappearance, and instantly declared her intention of starting out in search of her little niece. But it was now well past sunset and Mr. Moore persuaded her to wait until morning. His own horse was tired, but after an hour's rest Mr. Moore, accompanied by Aunt Pamela's nearest neighbor, started back toward Rosecrest, resolved to make a thorough search for Mary Lou, and not without hope that they might meet the little girl plodding along the highway, or that she might have returned to Rosecrest in Mr. Moore's absence.

Jasper, although it was midnight when Mr. Moore turned in at the drive leading to his home, was waiting for his master with the good news that, early in the evening, a messenger had arrived from Mr. Nelson saying that Mary Lou was safe at Nelson house and that early on the following morning she would be brought to Rosecrest. This was the best of news for the anxious men, and Mr. Moore was glad to go to rest knowing that his little cousin was safe in the house of a friend.

All the household at Rosecrest, excepting Rose Elinor, who had been fast asleep when the messenger arrived, had heard the good news, and Mammy Zella could hardly wait until morning to tell her young mistress, for that afternoon, when Rose Elinor had discovered that her cousin had not returned to Rosecrest, she had flown into such a temper that even Mammy Zella had lost patience and declared: "I mos' wish dat I could deal wid dis chile like she deserve! I reckon dat 'twould be de bes' t'ing in de worl' fer young Miss if I was 'lowed to gib her a good wallopin'." For Rose Elinor had screamed at the top of her voice:

"Find her! Don't stand around doing nothing! Find Mary Lou!"

For, at the knowledge that her cousin had vanished and could not be found, all Rose Elinor's anger against her cousin had instantly disappeared. She recalled Mary Lou's adoring eyes, as Mary Lou had declared Rose Elinor to be an "angel," and how delightful it had been to have a little girl for a companion who would do exactly as Rose Elinor wished her to do, and quite forgot that it was her own quick temper that was to blame for her cousin's running away.

It was in vain that Mammy Zella and the good-natured Clippy had endeavored to comfort her, and not until Mrs. Moore came hurrying to discover the reason for the shrieks that Mammy could not silence, and had told Rose Elinor that her father would surely bring Mary Lou safely home, was Rose Elinor persuaded to eat the dainty luncheon that Clippy hastened to bring from the kitchen, and to become once more the smiling little girl who, her mother declared, was the most warm-hearted child in Virginia.

Comforted by her mother's assurance that, when she awakened on the following morning, Mary Lou would be safely back at Rosecrest, Rose Elinor consented to make ready for her warm bath and to go to bed. But her thoughts centered about the little cousin and she remembered that Mary Lou had declared her to be an "angel." She remembered all that she had promised cousin—her own dolls; to dress the doll purchased in the Yorktown store, and to give Mary Lou "anything she wanted," and lying there in the big, shadowy chamber Rose Elinor could feel her face burn as she realized that she had not kept these promises; and that, unless Mary Lou came back to Rosecrest, she never could fulfill them.

CHAPTER V

MARY LOU AND THOMAS JEFFERSON

WHILE the search for Mary Lou was going forward the little girl herself was struggling through underbrush or along the rough banks of Wormeley Creek. In the time that had passed before it was discovered that she had not returned to Rosecrest with Rose Elinor and the search to find her began, Mary Lou had wandered a long distance from the grove of locust-trees that bordered the highway leading to Rosecrest.

Stumbling over the roots of trees, she clutched at the thorny shrubs and her thin little hands were soon scratched, and her muslin dress torn. As she was still wearing the heavy shoes in which she had arrived at Rosecrest her feet were well protected; she had worn a flower-wreathed straw hat that belonged to Rose Elinor, but in her first stumble over trailing vines it had flown from her head, and she did not know of her loss until it was useless to endeavor even to retrace her steps in search of it.

Now and then the little girl would stop and peer down the embankment and catch glimpses of what seemed smooth, grass-grown stretches along the border of the creek, and she was eager to reach this, sure that she could then go more quickly and soon reach Yorktown. She could not know that the green grass-covered marshland would sink beneath even so light a step as her own.

Not for a moment did Mary Lou forget "Lovely." Troubled and frightened as she was she managed, in all her falls and mishaps, to protect the doll from harm; and when she at last stood on the border of the marshland with her dress hanging in shreds, her hands torn by the cruel thorns, and her yellow hair snarled and full of bits of leaves and dust, "Lovely" was still as smiling, placid and uninjured as when the Yorktown storekeeper had handed the doll to its delighted owner.

"We will rest a little while, 'Lovely,'" she said aloud, smiling in spite of the fear that Rose Elinor might be angry at her because she had run away, and with a tired sigh the little girl sank back against the roots of an old beech-tree whose branches stretched out over the marsh.

It did not occur to Mary Lou that anyone would start in search of her, or that the wisest thing she could have done was to remain exactly where she had first stumbled in running away from Rose Elinor, and shout until someone came to her aid. For Great-aunt Pamela had firmly impressed upon her small niece that little girls should depend upon themselves, and make as little trouble as possible for older people. And now, as she rested beneath the big beech-tree,

Mary Lou's first thought was that the cousins at Rose-crest would think her a very careless and ungrateful child to be so long in finding her way back.

"I will say how very sorry I am, and I will promise never to displease Cousin Rose Elinor again," she thought humbly. "But I do wonder why she was angry at me for saying I was a Tory?" for Mary Lou had never been told that her father was fighting against England. Great-aunt Pamela, who had been taught from child-hood to be a loyal subject to England's king, was care-ful that her little niece should not discover that her father was a soldier in Washington's army; therefore it was no wonder that poor Mary Lou did not understand that she was a traitor to her own country in declaring herself a Tory.

The bank of Wormeley Creek was a very pleasant place to rest at noontime on that May day in 1781. The dogwood was still in bloom; the wild honeysuckle, clematis and sweetbrier filled the air with fragrance. A couple of mocking-birds, perched near by, were endeavoring to outsing each other; while from the underbrush came the musical calls of the cardinal bird and the woodland thrush. Mary Lou breathed in the sweet air, and the songs of the birds soothed and qui-eted her. She could hear the faint ripple of the stream as it flowed down to York River; and it was not long before the yellow head began to nod, and Mary Lou was fast asleep.

A few moments later a tall figure stepped from behind the beech-tree and started back in amazement as he discovered a little girl, with a doll resting across her lap, fast asleep.

The newcomer was tall, and his sandy hair waved back, under his soft hat, from a broad forehead. His features were well-formed and regular, and as he looked down at the tired child a smile crept about the stern mouth, and he whispered gently:

"A lost child!"

For a moment the tall man stood silent, thinking what it was best to do. He was staying at the house of Mr. Thomas Nelson, (that later was seized during the siege of Yorktown, and became the headquarters of the British general, Lord Cornwallis), and tempted by the fine weather, he had started out for a tramp down Wormeley Creek.

But it did not take him long to decide. To go on and leave the little girl there was out of the question. There was but one thing to do: he must carry her to Nelson house, nearly a mile distant, on the other side of the creek, and when she awoke discover where she lived, and see that she reached home safely; so, very gently he lifted the slender little figure in his arms, and retraced his steps along the way he had come, crossing the foot-bridge, and soon reaching the Nelson mansion, where his host came hurrying to meet him, exclaiming in surprise at the sight of the burden he carried:

"What has happened, Mr. Jefferson? Who is the child?" he exclaimed, but a warning gesture silenced him; for Mary Lou had not awakened, and Mr. Nelson nodded smilingly as he led the way up the steps of the fine mansion and into a large room, where Mr. Jefferson gently lowered Mary Lou to a broad sofa.

For a moment the two men, Mr. Thomas Nelson of Virginia, who was to follow Mr. Jefferson as Governor of Virginia, and Governor Thomas Jefferson, the author of America's "Declaration of Independence," stood looking down at the sleeping girl; then they tiptoed softly from the room and seated themselves on the shady porch, while Governor Jefferson told the story of discovering the child on the bank of Wormeley Creek.

"It is indeed fortunate that I happened to go in that direction; the little maid was at the very edge of the marsh, and might have endeavored to cross it and have been swallowed up, with nothing left to tell what had become of her."

Mr. Nelson soberly agreed. "I have no idea who the little girl can be," he said; "she must have wandered through the woods, for her dress is torn to shreds. But when she awakes she can tell us where she belongs, and we will send her safely home."

"Well, if her home be not too far distant, I will take her myself when I start for Rosecrest to-morrow morning," rejoined Mr. Jefferson. "I wish to talk with Mr. Moore about these new movements of Cornwallis. Do you not think Cornwallis may come in this direction?" he added; for, although the English still held New York, they had been baffled at all other points, and this invasion of the South was their last hope. France had come to America's assistance, and the British were determined to conquer in the South, and Earl Cornwallis, a brave English general, was in command of the army that had advanced into Virginia.

Mr. Nelson acknowledged that Cornwallis's progress was alarming. "But with young Lafayette at the head of our Virginia troops the fine English general will soon be driven into Chesapeake Bay!" he declared; and they again spoke of the little girl whom Mr. Jefferson had rescued.

"I will make sure that she is not disturbed," said Mr. Nelson; and left his guest and entered the house to give directions that no one should enter the room where Mary Lou had been taken.

The long, sunny hours slipped by and not until twilight did Mary Lou open her eyes. Her first thought was for "Lovely," and when she discovered that her treasured doll rested safely beside her, for Mr. Jefferson had taken good care that no harm should befall the doll, she gave a sigh of relief; then, still only half awake, she glanced up at the lofty ceiling of the big room; her eyes wandered to the fine mantelpiece of marble, carved into twisting vines, leaves, and bunches of grapes. Through the dimly lighted room she could see a wide doorway opening into a shadowy hall.

"It's a nice dream," she thought, sleepily, "but I wish I could dream Rose Elinor coming in that open doorway," and then suddenly she was wide awake, and remembered the woods, and the thorny bushes, and the big tree, and the song of the mocking-birds; and she sat up so quickly that "Lovely" fell from the sofa, without Mary Lou's noticing it, and rolled down on the thick fur rug, where she lay sprawled upon her face. For a moment Mary Lou had entirely forgotten "Lovely," and stared about her in amazement.

Suddenly there flashed into her mind a story that one of Great-aunt Pamela's servants had once told her of an enchanted castle, and of a little girl who had gone to sleep in her own home and awakened to find herself in a wonderful mansion, where an old witch lived who cast spells over little girls so that they became wicked fairies, and never escaped from the enchanted castle, but obeyed the old witch in whatever plans she might make.

"Oh! that is what has happened to me," Mary Lou whispered, too frightened to even remember "Lovely."

"I went to sleep close to a little river; and it was morning; and birds were singing; and there was no house in sight; and this is surely a castle, larger than Rosecrest; and it is nearly dark! What will I do if the witch finds me before I can escape?" And the little girl looked fearfully about, feeling sure that it would not do to run through the wide-open door into the big hall, as probably the witch was lurking there to seize her.

As she stood clutching the arm of the sofa Mary Lou heard a shrill voice call: "Down with all Tories! Down with all Tories!"

She could not, of course, know that it was Mrs. Nelson's parrot that had been carefully taught to repeat this phrase; she felt sure now that she was in the power of the wicked witch, and that all she could do was to keep out of her way as long as possible; and Mary Lou looked about the room for some way to escape. She discovered a closed door at the far end of the shadowy room and ran quickly toward it, turned the knob, and with an exclamation of surprise found herself gazing in at a room brilliantly lighted by tall candles in silver candlesticks that stood on a shining mahogany table, which reflected the glow of candle light.

There were big silver candelabras on the mantel, and silver sconces on the paneled walls of the room held wax candles whose glow sent gleams of light along the dark walls.

It was not often, in those anxious days toward the end of the American Revolution, that Mr. Thomas Jefferson, who was now Governor of Virginia, and later on to become President of the United States, and even in 1781 was famous as an upholder of democracy, found time to visit his friends, and the Nelsons had spread their table with their finest silver and china in his honor; great bunches of fragrant roses nodded from tall vases, and it was no wonder that Mary Lou, gazing in from the dim drawing-room, was now convinced that she had really awakened in an enchanted castle. In the story that the old negress had told her just such a banquet-room had been described, and the little girl softly closed the door behind her and stared about, holding her breath at the thought that at any moment the wicked witch and the fairies that did her bidding might appear.

As she stood there gazing at the soft glimmer of silver and glass, and, in spite of her fears, thinking it the most beautiful room in all the world, her glance rested on a glass bowl heaped up with strawberries that stood on a side table near the door by which she had entered the room. Beside it stood a tall glass pitcher filled with cream, and a silver cake-basket containing so many cakes, shaped like stars, and hearts, and diamonds, that for a moment Mary Lou's fears vanished, and she remembered only that she was hungry. She forgot the wicked witch, and tiptoed to the table. A big silver spoon rested near the berries, and there were glass saucers and a silver dish filled with powdered sugar. In an instant Mary Lou had filled a saucer with the ripe berries, dipped a spoon into the silver dish and heaped sugar upon them; with some little difficulty she managed to deluge the berries with thick cream from the tall pitcher, and then began to eat hungrily, helping herself to cakes with a liberal hand.

She had twice refilled her saucer when the opening of a door in the rear of the room caused her to look around and discover standing in the doorway a tall negro carrying a large silver tureen. At the same moment the door into the big hall opened, and Mrs. Nelson and Mr. Jefferson entered the dining-room, followed by Mr. Nelson and his daughter.

The negro nearly dropped the tureen; his eyes rolled wildly as he gazed at Mary Lou and then at his mistress, who was herself so surprised that she knew not what to do or say. But Mr. Jefferson quickly realized what had happened.

"It is the little maid I found by Wormeley Creek," he explained; and before Mary Lou could fly from the room as she meant to do, Mr. Jefferson was beside her, his friendly hand resting on the thin little shoulder, and his kind voice asked:

"Well, my little maid, did you know that I found you fast asleep near the creek and brought you all the way to Nelson house?"

"Isn't this an enchanted castle?" responded Mary Lou in a whisper, looking up at the pleasant face that smiled down upon her in so friendly a manner.

"Why, no; it is the home of Mr. Thomas Nelson," explained Mr. Jefferson gravely. "Let me introduce you to Mrs. Nelson," he continued, "if you will tell me your name."

"My name is Mary Lou Abbott; and, if you please, I must go to Rosecrest as soon as I can," Mary Lou responded anxiously, and then with a wail of despair, "Oh! 'Lovely'! 'Lovely'! I've lost 'Lovely'!"

CHAPTER VI

ROSE ELINOR'S NEW RESOLVES

ROSE ELINOR was up at an unusually early hour on the morning after Mary Lou's disappearance, and Mammy Zella, beaming with smiles, came hurrying to tell her young mistress that Mary Lou was safe at the house of Mr. Nelson, and that very soon she would arrive at Rosecrest. Before Mammy Zella could speak Rose Elinor was out of bed, running across the room toward her, calling out, "Where's Mary Lou? Did my father bring her home?"

Mammy's face grew stern. "Yo' lissen, Miss Rose Elinor——" she began; but instantly Rose imagined that Mary Lou had not been found, and she flung herself against Mammy, striking at her angrily, and again crying out, "Find her! I tell you, find her!"

Mammy grasped the girl's hands and held her at arm's length.

"Yo' cousin is foun'. Ain' yo' 'shamed, Rose Elinor? Ain' yo' shame' yo'sef, to hit yo' own ole mammy. I'se gwine to tell Massa Moore ob yo'; an' I'se gwine to tell Massa Thomas Jeff'son ob yo'. An' I'se gwine to go off an' leab yo'. I shure is!"

It was seldom anyone even reproved the little mistress of Rosecrest; and as she listened to Mammy a smile crept over Rose Elinor's face. How funny Mammy Zella talked, she thought, a little wonderingly.

"Yo' can laf, if yo' wants to, Rose Elinor, but yo' don' act de way a Virginny young lady orter behabe," declared Mammy soberly. "Yo' cousin, Mary Lou, am safe an' soun' at Massa Nelson's house; an' dey plan to fetch her ober dis mawnin'; an' now yo' gwine to hab yo' bath."

Rose Elinor's smile faded at Mammy Zella's announcement that she did not behave as a young lady of Virginia was expected to behave; it recalled the fact that she had, for a time, forgotten her promises to Mary Lou; and she was very quiet and thoughtful as Mammy Zella prepared her bath and brushed her hair. Nothing could have been said to Rose Elinor that would have had so good an effect as to tell her that she fell below the standards expected of a young lady of Virginia. And Rose Elinor made another resolve that morning: Not even Mammy, she firmly decided, should again have reason to say that Rose Elinor Moore did not behave as a young lady of Virginia should.

"Mary Lou shall see that I keep every promise I make. And I'll show Mammy that I can be as fine a young lady as my own mother," she resolved, quite sure that no one could be nearer perfection than that.

At breakfast Mr. Moore questioned Rose as to the manner in which she and Mary Lou had become separated on the previous day.

"I don't know, Father. I hid away from Clippy, just for fun, and when I came back to the highway the carriage was gone. I supposed Mary Lou was in the carriage," she explained; for she had again resolved that no one must discover that her cousin was a traitor to America.

Mr. Moore's face lightened as Rose Elinor told of hiding from Clippy. "I am glad that Mary Lou did not really start out for Aunt Pamela's," he said, "but what made you think she had started off alone on such a journey?"

"Well, Father, if Mary Lou thought I had run away from her, she might have started off to go back to Great-aunt Pamela's," replied Rose Elinor.

"I see. But I hope after this, my dear, that you will never let Mary Lou even imagine that a little maid of Virginia would run away from a guest," her father rejoined.

Rose Elinor's face flushed uncomfortably; for a moment she was tempted to push back her chair from the table and run crying from the room, sure that if she did this her mother would come running after her and promise her anything she might ask if she would only smile again. But Mammy's words, "Yo' don' act de way a Virginny young lady orter behabe," were still fresh in her thoughts, and her own resolve now kept her silent for a moment; then she said slowly:

"I forgot Mary Lou was a guest."

"Of course you did, darling child," her mother instantly declared. And before her father could speak, Rose added:

"But I won't forget again."

Mr. Moore looked a little surprised, but he was greatly pleased and nodded approvingly.

"Well, it is great good fortune that Mary Lou is safe. I hope Mr. Jefferson may ride over from Nelson house to-day," he added, and Rose Elinor's face brightened.

"That will be splendid! Then he can talk to Mary Lou," she exclaimed.

Mr. and Mrs. Moore both smiled, thinking their little daughter eager to make her cousin acquainted with the great Virginian, and not imagining that Rose Elinor was earnestly hoping that Mr. Jefferson could quickly convert Mary Lou into a loyal American.

After breakfast Rose Elinor went up to the platform on the top of the house. From there she could look along the road over which Mary Lou would come to Rosecrest.

"I'll give her my dolls just as soon as she gets here, and we will begin to dress the new doll this very afternoon," she thought eagerly, looking off to the distant highway.

"There she comes! There she comes!" she exclaimed a moment later as she discovered something coming along the road. It was still too far away for her to make out if it was someone on horseback or a carriage, and it seemed to move very slowly.

"Oh, why doesn't it come faster!" Rose Elinor exclaimed impatiently. "Whoever it is, it moves as slowly as Great-aunt Pamela's old mule 'Solomon.'"

But gradually the distant conveyance, for Rose Elinor soon discovered it to be some sort of a carriage, crept into a nearer view; and, with a gasp of surprise, Rose Elinor saw that it really was Great-aunt Pamela's old gray mule, driven by Uncle Peter; and in the small cart she could see a nodding head surmounted by a tall black bonnet.

"It is Great-aunt Pamela Fairfax Cutting!" declared the astonished girl; and instantly she became afraid that Great-aunt Pamela had come after Mary Lou.

"She shall not take her away. I will not let her. Oh! Some way I must not let Great-aunt Pamela discover that Mary Lou has been found," thought Rose Elinor, sure that her Great-aunt Pamela could have no other object in coming to Rosecrest than to take Mary Lou home with her.

But as the little girl's eyes rested on the slowly moving vehicle she again exclaimed in surprise. For on the road behind old "Solomon," came Mr. Nelson's fine coach drawn by four black horses. For a moment it seemed to Rose Elinor that this fine equipage, whose horses came on at such a pace, would surely run over the little cart that still kept the centre of the highway, and Rose Elinor clutched at the railing which surrounded the platform in silent terror, fearing that the coachman might not see the old mule and that in another moment Great-aunt Pamela might be crushed under the feet of the black horses. But a moment later

she saw the coach come to a sudden stop; the big horses were turned quickly, so that it was plainly evident
that the coachman did not intend to dash past the
small cart. The door of the coach swung open and a tall
figure stepped out and hurried toward the cart.

"Perhaps it is Mr. Thomas Jefferson," thought Rose
Elinor, "and if it is, Great-aunt Pamela will surely not
speak to him, for she declares him to be a traitor to
King George."

And this was exactly what did happen. Mary Lou,
peering out from the window of the coach, saw Mr. Jefferson, hat in hand, approach the shabby little cart,
and, with a low bow, salute Great-aunt Pamela. She
heard him ask if Miss Cutting would not do him the
honor to take a seat in Mr. Nelson's coach and ride in
his company to Rosecrest; and she saw Great-aunt
Pamela, without a word of response to Mr. Jefferson,
lean forward and tap Uncle Pete smartly on the shoulder, and heard her say, "Peter! Drive on! Why are you
stopping to take the dust from the horses of a traitor
to King George!" And instantly Uncle Peter flourished
his whip, old Solomon started forward, and Mr. Jefferson was left standing in the road. Then he slowly
returned to the coach and bade the driver follow the
cart at as slow a pace as possible.

"Do not, by any chance, come near enough to Miss
Cutting's carriage to annoy her," he said gravely, and
took his seat again beside Mary Lou.

"If you please, sir, that is my Great-aunt Pamela," said Mary Lou; "and, while there is not room for me beside her in the cart, I could, if you please, walk along the road beside her."

Mr. Jefferson turned a friendly smile upon his little companion as he responded: "I am sure your aunt would prefer that you should ride, even with as loyal an American as Thomas Jefferson, rather than walk on this dusty highway. I am sorry indeed that the aunt of so brave an American as your father is a Tory."

Mary Lou's blue eyes widened in surprise. "Is not my dear father a Tory?" she asked anxiously.

"Heaven forbid! Why, child, even at your age you should know how unfairly England and King George have treated the American Colonies, with no thought for America excepting to derive profit from the sufferings of its people. Not allowing us to have a word to say as to what laws should govern us, and disregarding all our petitions. And Virginians had loved England; we do not forget that our grandfathers were Englishmen," he concluded, a little sadly, quite forgetting his small companion as he recalled the long war for American rights that was now so nearly at an end.

Mary Lou gave a little sigh. She had hoped to discover just what a Tory was, and after a moment she ventured to ask:

"Would my father want me to be a Tory?"

Mr. Jefferson leaned toward the anxious-eyed child and spoke quickly:

"My dear little girl, your father is willing to give his life that you may grow up in freedom; that no far-off king shall have power to make unjust laws through which you would suffer. Remember this. 'Is life so dear, or peace so sweet, as to be purchased at the price of chains and slavery? As for me, give me liberty or give me death,'" and as Mr. Jefferson repeated these words of his friend Patrick Henry, he again seemed to forget the little girl by his side.

Mary Lou asked no more questions as the coach, moving so slowly in order not to overtake "Miss Cutting's carriage," that it seemed hardly to move at all, crept along toward Rosecrest. But she had quickly made up her mind that if her father was fighting against America's enemies, and if those enemies were called "Tories," she could no longer be a Tory.

She now understood why Rose Elinor had seemed angry because of her declaration of loyalty to King George. "But why did Rose Elinor say she had hoped I would be a Tory?" thought the puzzled child. "I will tell her that I am the daughter of a loyal American."

Rose Elinor was not the only one who watched the progress of the little cavalcade along the road to Rose-crest, and when old Solomon crawled up the driveway Mr. and Mrs. Moore were on the steps to welcome Aunt Pamela Cutting. Mr. Jefferson had told the coachman to stop at the entrance to the drive, where he lifted Mary Lou from the coach, saying, "We will walk up from here," and taking the little girl by the hand, they walked slowly through the beautiful gardens toward the house.

"No, nephew! I will not cross your threshold until you repent of your traitorous opinions," responded Aunt Pamela, as Mr. Moore endeavored to persuade her to leave the cart. "I came only to be assured that Mary Lou is in safety," and the mistaken old lady looked sternly at the friendly faces of Mr. and Mrs. Moore, who were so eager to welcome her to Rosecrest.

"Yes, Aunt Pamela, Mary Lou is safe. Here she comes up the path with Mr. Jefferson," said Mrs. Moore. "He has kindly accompanied her home from the house of Mr. Nelson, where she spent the night."

At that moment Mary Lou had discovered her Great-aunt Pamela, and, drawing her hand from the clasp of her new friend, she ran quickly toward the donkey-cart.

"Great-aunt Pamela! Great-aunt Pamela! Here I am," she called, and Miss Cutting's stern face softened as she turned toward the little girl. But she did not forget what she felt was her first "duty" toward her niece, and in a firm voice she responded to Mary Lou's eager greeting:

"Is that the proper manner for a loyal Tory girl to greet her aunt? Did I not teach you properly? Or have you forgotten your manners?"

Mary Lou's smile disappeared. She took a backward step and made her best curtsey, and then, half fearfully, but looking bravely at her Great-aunt Pamela, she responded in clear tones:

"If you please, Great-aunt Pamela, my father is an American soldier, so I cannot be a Tory girl any longer."

"Turn the mule, Peter!" commanded Miss Cutting; and, without another word to the little group of people, all of whom were eager to be friendly with the mistaken old lady, Great-aunt Pamela's donkey-cart moved down the driveway and disappeared behind the thick hedges that enclosed the garden.

CHAPTER VII

ROSE ELINOR AND THE BEADED BAG

MR. JEFFERSON did not approach the porch until Miss Pamela Fairfax Cutting's "carriage" had turned into the highway; then he walked slowly toward the house, and Mr. and Mrs. Moore hastened to welcome him, while Rose Elinor, who had hurried down-stairs, took possession of Mary Lou after a wondering glance at her little cousin's fine dress and pretty hat.

For Mary Lou no longer wore the torn white muslin and thick shoes in which she had arrived at Mr. Nelson's. As soon as Mrs. Nelson had listened to the little girl's story of her wanderings along Wormeley Creek, and when "Lovely" had been restored to its delighted owner, Mary Lou was taken to a pleasant upper chamber by Mrs. Nelson's maid; a big chest was opened, and Mary Lou gazed in wonder as dress after dress, all for a girl of about her own size, was taken out. Not only dresses, but the daintiest of underwear, stockings, slippers, and, from a round hat-box in a closet, the maid brought a wide-rimmed, flat-crowned hat of fine white straw, trimmed with delicate pink ribbon.

"Jes' ter show yo', Missy," said the smiling maid. "I reckon yo're to w'ar it ter-morrow!"

Mary Lou was told to select the dress she liked best, and was soon quite a different little girl in appearance from the ragged, frightened child whom Mr. Jefferson had introduced to Mrs. Nelson in the candle-lit dining-room of Nelson house.

Mary Lou selected a dress of pale pink dimity, with little white rosebuds embroidered upon it. The dress had a round collar of lace, with tiny ruffles of lace on the sleeves. Her underwear was of the sheerest of linen, and her white stockings were silk, with kid ankle-ties.

"Dey might hab been made fer yo', Missy; dey sho' might," declared the admiring maid, tying back Mary Lou's carefully brushed yellow hair with a wide ribbon of pink silk.

"All dese clo'es belong ter my young miss, wot got married an' went off ter lib in Richmon'," she explained, as she led Mary Lou, holding "Lovely" more firmly than ever, back to the dining-room, where she was lifted to a chair beside Mr. Jefferson, and, in spite of the saucers of berries and the cakes that she had eaten, found herself quite ready to enjoy the salad and a new supply of berries.

Mary Lou hastened to tell Rose Elinor the story of all that had befallen her since the two cousins had been separated in the woods on the previous day. They had seated themselves on the upper step of the porch, after Rose Elinor had made her curtsey to Mr. Jefferson as he came up with her father and mother, and she now listened eagerly to all that Mary Lou had to say.

"And Mrs. Nelson gave me a note for your mother, Rose Elinor," and from a square beaded bag which hung over her arm, Mary Lou took out a folded paper.

Rose Elinor instantly exclaimed about the bag. "It has a peacock wrought in all colors of beads, Mary Lou! I never saw anything so pretty," she declared; and instantly Mary Lou had slipped the ribbons from her arm and, smiling with delight, held the bag toward her cousin.

"Take it, dear Rose Elinor," she said eagerly. "Mrs. Nelson said it was truly mine; so I may give it you," and she thrust the beaded bag into her cousin's hands.

For a moment Rose Elinor hesitated. For Mary Lou to bestow so beautiful a gift before Rose Elinor could fulfill her own promises did not exactly please her; but it was a wonderful bag, and Mary Lou's pleading eyes could not be resisted. "Thank you," she responded, a little stiffly; and then as Mary Lou's eager smile faded, Rose Elinor quickly added, "I will always keep it, and I think you are very good to give it to me," and she leaned forward impulsively and kissed her cousin's cheek.

Mary Lou's face brightened with happiness, her eyes shone, and for the moment she felt herself the happiest little girl in Virginia; and when, a moment later, Mrs. Moore appeared in the doorway, she thought there could be no more attractive picture than the two cousins, Rose Elinor, with her dark curls and soft dark eyes, and blue-eyed Mary Lou, who was gazing at her cousin adoringly.

"A companion is just what Rose Elinor needed," Mrs. Moore decided, well pleased that Mary Lou showed so much affection for her cousin.

After Mrs. Moore had read the letter from Mrs. Nelson that Mary Lou handed to her, she turned smilingly toward Mary Lou.

"Mrs. Nelson writes to say that, as her daughter's clothing fits you so exactly, she wishes you to have a number of the dresses, the underwear, and the shoes, and says she has had them packed and will send them over. I think you must have made a very pleasant impression, my dear," she said approvingly.

Before Mary Lou could respond Rose Elinor jumped up and, stamping her foot angrily, exclaimed:

"Mary Lou sha'n't have anybody's old things! She sha'n't! *I* am going to give her things. Nobody else is going to give her dresses!"

For a moment Mrs. Moore's face grew anxious and troubled; then, as usual, her little daughter's temper seemed to the indulgent mother only another evidence of Rose Elinor's generous nature, and she said indulgently:

"Dear child, you shall indeed give your cousin whatever you please," and instantly Rose Elinor was again all smiles.

But Mary Lou's face was very serious as she stood looking first at her beloved cousin and then at Mrs. Moore.

"You don't want the old dresses, do you, Mary Lou?" declared Rose eagerly.

For a brief moment Mary Lou did not answer. Then, in a voice hardly above a whisper, she said, "I told Mrs. Nelson I would wear the things. She did not scold me for going into the dining-room and eating berries and cakes; she said it was of no consequence; and she came up-stairs after I was in bed and kissed me good-night. If you please, Rose Elinor, I must keep the dresses and wear them," and Mary Lou looked pleadingly toward Rose Elinor, hoping her cousin would promptly agree. But as she turned toward Rose Elinor she was suddenly struck in the face by the bead bag that Rose hurled at her, saying:

"Then keep your old bag. I don't want it," and fled into the house.

Mary Lou put her hand to her face with a sharp cry, for the bag had struck her with such force as to cut her cheek. Mrs. Moore ran toward her, and, putting an arm about the little girl, endeavored to comfort her, saying:

"Dear, Rose Elinor did not mean to hurt you, Mary Lou. It was only because she wanted to do everything for you."

Mary Lou choked back her sobs. Great-aunt Pamela had small patience with "cry-babies," and Mary Lou had long ago learned that to cry over one's hurts is of small use. And now she kept back the tears, although she could not speak. Mrs. Moore led her up to her chamber and gently bathed the hurt cheek, speaking of Rose Elinor's impulsive, warm nature, and telling Mary Lou again that Rose did not mean to hurt her.

The bell rang for luncheon, and Mrs. Moore suddenly remembered that Mr. Thomas Jefferson was their guest, and bidding Mary Lou to follow her to the dining-room, she hurried from the room, leaving the little girl alone.

"I 'most wish I could have stayed with Great-aunt Pamela," thought Mary Lou. "I knew just what Great-aunt wanted me to do, and I don't know what Rose Elinor wants me to do," and the puzzled little girl looked helplessly about the room, and her glance fell on the box that had journeyed with her in the donkey-cart from Great-aunt Pamela's.

As she looked at it her face brightened. In that box were her own things, and if Cousin Rose Elinor did not want her to wear the fine dresses that Mrs. Nelson had given her, why, Mary Lou decided that she would put on her very own things.

"But I will not send back what Mrs. Nelson gave me; and sometimes I will wear them, because I promised to. But Rose Elinor will be well pleased to see me in my own things, and will no longer be angry at me," she thought hopefully, quite forgetting her bruised cheek as she opened the leather-covered box.

As Mary Lou drew out a plainly made frock of coarse gray linen, a little square package, wrapped in white paper and sealed with crimson wax, fell to the floor. Mary Lou picked it up and with an exclamation of surprise read the inscription: "To Lieutenant-General Earl Cornwallis—or to any officer in the service of King George." Below this inscription was written:

"My dear Great-niece: If you find yourself in danger, this letter will win you protection. Your Aunt Pamela Fairfax Cutting."

For a few moments Mary Lou sat on the floor beside the box, holding the package in her hand, and wondering about it; then, with a little smile, she put it back in the leather-covered box, under a pile of garments, saying to herself that Great-aunt Pamela could not know that at Rosecrest a little girl would always be quite safe. And now she hastened to slip on the gray dress; to put on a pair of thick shoes, exactly like the ones she had worn on her arrival; and in a few minutes she was again dressed as she had been when Rose Elinor first saw her; and, quite forgetting the white-covered package that she had found in her leather-covered box, Mary Lou made her way to the dining-room.

Mr. Moore smiled a welcome to the timid little girl as she entered the room.

"You are to sit beside Governor Jefferson, my dear," he said. "But where is Rose Elinor?"

At that moment his little daughter entered the room, made a pretty curtsey to Mr. Jefferson, and slipped into the seat beside him, the one her father had told Mary Lou to take.

"Take the chair next to Rose Elinor, Mary Lou," said Mrs. Moore, who now felt anxious over the little girl's bruised cheek and her change of dress.

But before Mary Lou could obey this suggestion, Mr. Moore said laughingly:

"No, my dear, I think Mary Lou is to sit beside Mr. Jefferson. I am sure Rose Elinor desires her cousin to have the seat of honor," and he bowed smilingly toward his distinguished guest.

Rose Elinor did not even glance at Mary Lou as she gave her the seat; and Mary Lou, who had looked up, hopeful of at least an approving smile when Rose Elinor should see that she was wearing her very own clothes, again grew sober and wistful-eyed.

Mr. Moore was too greatly interested in Mr. Jefferson's conversation to give further attention to the little girls.

"Lafayette writes me from Richmond that he is in the greatest need of arms, and that he must have prompt assistance if his troops are to withstand Cornwallis," said Mr. Jefferson. "The British are well mounted and well supplied with all necessities. We must at once get aid for our troops or Virginia will be taken by the enemy."

And as Governor Jefferson said good-bye to Mary Lou, who in the ugly dress and with her bruised and swollen cheek, looked very unlike the well-dressed little girl who had ridden with him that morning from Nelson house, he said smilingly:

"Be sure and remember, little maid, the cause for which your brave father is fighting. And do not forget what Mrs. Nelson's parrot told you.

"'Down with all Tories,'" Mary Lou repeated soberly, and Mr. Jefferson repeated the words after her, and then entered the coach which was to convey him to Charlottesville and drove away.

CHAPTER VIII

DEFYING A WITCH

BEFORE the cousins returned to the house Rose Elinor had poured out the story of her difficulties and resolves to Mary Lou.

"Sometimes I truly think there are two of me," she declared earnestly, "because, of course, a young lady, and I am past eleven, never gets angry or does mean things or forgets a promise; and, Mary Lou," and Rose Elinor clasped her cousin's arm tightly, "I do all those things before I remember that I am a young lady of Virginia. But I guess I will never forget again; anyway not until your poor cheek is well!" And Rose Elinor's face flushed with shame as she looked at the bruise on her cousin's face.

Before the two little girls returned to the house they had agreed that some wicked fairy had, as Mary Lou suggested, "put an enchantment" upon Rose Elinor.

"Of course that is it," declared Mary Lou earnestly, "because you do not want to get angry, and you never would do anything yourself that wasn't right and kind! Just see how lovely you've been to me," and Mary Lou's blue eyes rested so admiringly upon her cousin that Rose

Elinor, although she felt herself too old to really believe in fairies, began to think Mary Lou was right.

"You must remember it is a bad fairy trying to make you into a witch," urged the younger girl, "and you must say a charm against her every time you begin to feel angry. Old Linny told me about it. Oh, Rose Elinor! Isn't it lucky I remember the charm? This is the way it goes:

> " 'One—and—Two—and—Three!
> Witch, I am free.
> Three—and—Two—and—One!
> Witch! Begone.' "

Mary Lou repeated the charm solemnly, and Rose Elinor said the words over after her until she was sure that she would remember them.

"Of course, just the very minute you begin to think that the witch is trying to make you angry you must say the charm," cautioned Mary Lou, "and you must be sure to shut your eyes when you say the charm."

Rose Elinor laughed delightedly at her little cousin's solemn voice, but she was quite ready to promise; and she led the way to her own room, where her four dolls, with an entire bureau to hold their fine clothes, were promptly bestowed on the delighted Mary Lou.

Mammy Zella insisted on bathing Mary Lou's cheek with a soothing lotion, now and then shaking her head and muttering to herself as she looked toward Rose Elinor; for Clippy had been near at hand when Rose Elinor had hurled the beaded bag at her cousin; and Mammy Zella began to fear "dat som' wicked ole witch's a-clutchin' after young Rose Elinor."

But the afternoon passed happily for the entire household. Rose Elinor had now fulfilled her promises to Mary Lou. She also had a "charm" that she hoped would prevent her from "behabin' de way no Virginny young lady oughter behabe"; and there was nothing to trouble her as she and Mary Lou carried the dolls to the platform on the roof, where Rose Elinor pointed out to her cousin the glimpse of the village of Yorktown; and, across the river, Gloucester Point could be seen.

"We will go over there some day and take our luncheon and stay all day," said Rose Elinor. "Perhaps Black Jasper can drive us over to Yorktown to-morrow, and we will cross the river to Gloucester Point. Clippy can go with us, and we will take 'Lovely' and your other dolls, and I will take my work," she added.

"But does your mother not wish us to help her with sewing, or in gathering the early herbs for drying?" responded Mary Lou soberly, recalling Great-aunt Pamela's constant industry.

Rose Elinor shook her head laughingly. "What a queer idea! Why, I only do what I please," she said. "Do you not despise Great-aunt Pamela for making you work like a servant, and for teaching you to be a Tory?" she questioned.

Mary Lou's face clouded. But she did not hesitate. "No, Rose Elinor. Great-aunt Pamela wished me to grow up a useful woman. She said so every day. But I am indeed sorry she is so mistaken as to think it right to be a Tory," she replied, looking anxiously toward her cousin. As her glance rested on Rose Elinor a little smile crept about her mouth, for Rose Elinor's eyes were closed and she was whispering to herself. A moment later she looked up at her cousin smilingly.

"I do believe the charm is going to work," she declared, and the little girls both laughed delightedly.

Mr. and Mrs. Moore approved of Rose Elinor's plan for a visit to Gloucester Point, and it was decided they should go on the following day.

"It will be the first day of June and a pleasant way to begin the month," said Mr. Moore. "Jasper can leave the horses at Yorktown and take you across the river in my boat. With Jasper and Clippy to look after them they will be safe enough," he added, turning to his wife, and Mrs. Moore smilingly agreed. That night, when Mary Lou was quite alone in her large, pleasant chamber, she decided that, if a wicked witch really was trying to make Rose Elinor unhappy, a good fairy was surely keeping watch over herself. "For whatever happens to me, even if it seems bad, comes out all right," she thought, recalling her adventures at Nelson house, and remembering that her bruised cheek had made Rose Elinor confide in her. She was looking forward to the pleasure of the coming day's excursion with her cousin. "Perhaps Rose

Elinor will tell me what she meant when she said that she hoped I was a Tory," she thought. And then Mary Lou suddenly remembered the square white package addressed to Earl Cornwallis, that was hidden in her leather-covered box, and again she smiled to think that even Great-aunt Pamela could think of any harm befalling a little girl who was fortunate enough to live at Rosecrest. Mary Lou could not even imagine that before another night the possession of a letter addressed to the commander of the king's troops was to rescue her cousin and herself from a great danger.

The next morning was clear and pleasant, the air filled with the fragrance of June roses and blossoming honeysuckle, while a cool little breeze from the river crept over the fields and woods, bringing odors of wild flowers and growing plants. At breakfast Rose Elinor talked eagerly of the plans she had made for the day's pleasure.

"Clippy, you are to bring all the dolls," she said.

"I will take 'Lovely' myself," said Mary Lou a little anxiously, for, pleased as she was with the family of dolls that her cousin had so generously bestowed upon her, no other doll could ever seem quite as dear as "Lovely," and she knew that she would enjoy the day much better if she herself carried "Lovely."

"All right," responded her cousin, and Clippy brought down the other dolls and established them on the carriage seat opposite the cousins.

"It's splendid to go for all day," declared Rose Elinor.

Mary Lou nodded her head vigorously as she replied:

"Great-aunt Pamela would hardly believe me if I should tell her that I have not set a stitch or done a useful act since coming to Rosecrest. Why, Rose Elinor! I never played in all my life before!" and the little girl, whose nine years had been passed without playmates or amusements, looked gravely at the laughing face of her wonderful cousin who had known only happiness.

"Well! You are going to play now. You are going to have a good time every day!" Rose Elinor responded quickly. "And Mammy Zella says that you must drink cream and take naps, so as to get some flesh on your bones," and an anxious little frown showed on Rose Elinor's smooth forehead as her glance rested on Mary Lou's thin cheeks.

Black Jasper chose the upper road which led through cultivated fields and woods of lofty pines, laurels, and other forest trees, which cast a refreshing shade as they rode along. Rose Elinor was surprised when Mary Lou confessed that, until Mrs. Nelson had introduced her to the Governor of Virginia, she had never even heard the name of Thomas Jefferson mentioned.

"Why, my father says that Mr. Jefferson is the greatest of Virginians, and one of the leaders of the American Revolution. He wrote the Declaration of Independence," declared Rose Elinor, quite sure that now Mary Lou would realize the importance of her new friend.

"What is that?" Mary Lou questioned calmly.

Rose Elinor regarded her cousin with a pitying expression. "I do declare, Mary Lou, if you hadn't come to live at Rosecrest you would never have really known that you were an American. The 'Declaration' is a fine paper, written by Mr. Jefferson, because Congress asked him to write it, saying that America will make her own laws and is an independent nation."

Mary Lou did not seem much surprised by what her cousin told her of her new friend. "He was very kind to me, and told me about my father, and Mr. Jefferson cured me of being a Tory," she responded calmly, much as if she were telling of being cured of a toothache.

"I knew he would. Oh, Mary Lou, wasn't it fortunate that Mr. Jefferson found you? You see, if anybody else had discovered you, you might not have found out about the reason your father is a soldier."

Before Mary Lou could make any rejoinder a turn of the road brought them in sight of Yorktown Village, and across the river, which is much narrower at that point, was Gloucester Point, and Rose Elinor eagerly called Mary Lou to look from the carriage window and pointed across the stream.

"That is where we are going, Mary Lou! And from that high bank we can look way down the river, and on the shore are tiny flat stones that we can 'skip' on the water."

In her eagerness to point out their destination Rose Elinor, kneeling on the carriage seat, leaned so far out of the open window that she lost her balance, and had not Mary Lou instantly clutched her dress with both hands and Clippy sprung to her assistance, she would have fallen head-first from the window.

Clippy's shriek, as she drew her young mistress back into the carriage, caused Jasper to bring his horses to a sudden stop, and he looked wildly around to discover what had happened.

"My hat, Jasper, I lost it from the window," explained Rose Elinor, and Clippy, chuckling to herself over what she termed "Young Missy's grown-uppiness," went back along the road to rescue the hat, and Rose Elinor smoothed back her curls, put on her hat and, without a word in regard to what might indeed have proved a serious accident, explained, "You know, Mary Lou, that if you throw a flat, thin stone in the right way it will 'skip' over the water."

Mary Lou picked up "Lovely" from the floor of the carriage, where the doll had fallen when Mary Lou had sprung to grab her cousin, and as she gazed at her treasure tears came quickly into her eyes, for "Lovely's" nose had been broken by the fall, and for a few moments the little girl could not speak. But Rose Elinor talked on, telling of the wild strawberries they would be sure to find at Gloucester Point and of a grove of oaks where it would be pleasant to eat luncheon; she was so vexed at her own clumsiness in leaning too far out the window, to even remember that but for her cousin and Clippy's prompt assistance she might have been seriously hurt. But later on Rose Elinor remembered this.

The horses were left at the stable of the "Swan" Tavern, and Jasper with the basket of luncheon and Clippy, carrying the four dolls in her arms, led the way down toward the wharf where a boat belonging to Mr. Moore was fastened. Jasper and Clippy had both been warned by Mr. Moore not to lose sight for a moment of the two girls, and Clippy's head turned so often to make sure that they were close at hand that Rose Elinor laughed delightedly, and Mary Lou almost forgot poor "Lovely's" mishap in her cousin's laughter, and in watching Clippy's anxious face.

It did not take long for the little party to reach Gloucester Point. Jasper carried the basket to the shade of the big oaks and, lighting his corn-cob pipe with a sigh of relief, established himself for a comfortable hour of freedom.

The June sunshine grew from a pleasant morning warmth into midday heat. Jasper's pipe went out, his head nodded and he "los' myse'f," as he afterward confessed. Clippy, holding the damaged doll in her lap while the other four were placed in a row beside her, kept her sharp eyes on the little girls, assuring herself that she would not let them go beyond her ability to call them back. She did not know when she went to sleep, but when Jasper's voice, in her very ear, demanded:

"Hy'are! Yo' Clippy! Ain' yo' a disg'ace! Whar dose chillun?" she jumped up so quickly that again the unfortunate "Lovely" tumbled headlong, and, looking wildly about, repeated Jasper's question.

"Whar dose chillun?" For there was no trace along the quiet shore of either of the little girls.

CHAPTER IX

DANGER

ROSE ELINOR had been the one to discover that Clippy was napping, and at once a plan entered her head to puzzle the faithful servant, and at the same time amuse her cousin and herself.

"Come on, Mary Lou. Let's creep up that bank behind Clippy and hide. She will wake up in a minute and when she finds we have disappeared she'll make a great fuss."

Mary Lou promptly agreed, and the two little girls crept up the bank and crouched down behind some low-growing shrubs. They had just concealed themselves when Jasper came striding down, and in a moment they heard him berating Clippy because she had gone to sleep and heard Clippy respond: "De Lawd knows I nebber know'd I was asleep 'til I wakes up."

The cousins had hard work to restrain their laughter as they watched Clippy and Jasper running about the shore, peering into the boat and stopping every few minutes to blame each other because the girls could not be found.

"I tells you, Jasper, dose chillun is whar de lunch baskit is," they heard Clippy declare, and saw Jasper start off at once in the direction of the oak grove, closely followed by Clippy.

"I wish we were near the luncheon basket," said Rose Elinor laughingly, "for I am hungry as a bear."

"I am hungry as two bears," declared Mary Lou.

"We'll go down to the shore and begin to skip stones, as if we had been there all the time, and when they come back to look for us again we will act surprised, just as if we did not know what they were talking about," said Rose Elinor.

"Sshh," whispered Mary Lou. "Here they come!" for she heard steps close at hand, and was sure it must be Jasper and Clippy. But at that very instant a crouching figure rose from behind the bushes and stood directly in front of the surprised and frightened children.

"Keep quiet," he said threateningly. "If either of you call or scream 'twill be the last of you," and he touched the handle of a big hunting-knife that swung from his belt, with a warning gesture. "And answer my questions quickly."

The man was tall and thin; his face was covered by a heavy beard and he was dressed in blouse and trousers of gray homespun with high boots. Beside the knife, a pair of pistols rested in his belt, and his face was shaded by the broad rim of an old felt hat. It was no wonder the little cousins were frightened by this threatening figure, and crouched close together, not knowing what evil fate might be in store for them.

"If You Call or Scream, 'Twill Be the Last of You."

"Answer quickly, I have no time to lose," he continued, kneeling down in front of them so that anyone approaching from the shore or coming down the slope could not see him.

"You have just come from Yorktown?" he questioned sharply, his eyes fixed upon Rose Elinor, who nodded her response, too frightened to speak.

"And Jefferson was at Mr. Moore's house yesterday. Do you know the Moores?"

Rose Elinor nodded again.

"Where was Jefferson bound?"

"Charlottesville," whispered the frightened child.

"Your name?" demanded the questioner.

"Rose Elinor Moore, and if my father—" but the man raised a threatening hand, although a little smile crept about his lips.

"That's good news. Now what did Jefferson and your father talk about?"

"Cornwallis and Lafayette," responded Rose Elinor.

"Ah-ha! This is luck! I think you young ladies had better come with me," he said, rising to his feet. "Come along, no time to lose!" and he grasped Mary Lou's shoulder and lifted her from the ground, and at that moment Rose Elinor, defying his warning, screamed at the top of her voice: "Jasper! Clippy!"

In an instant the man seized her, clapped his hand over her mouth, and telling Mary Lou to keep close beside him, ran along the bank for a short distance, then with a quick look around to make sure that no one was observing him, he pushed aside a growth of laurel behind which was a dark opening leading into the cliff-like bank. "Go in," he commanded Mary Lou sternly, and the little girl entered the cave, closely followed by the crouching figure of the man carrying Rose Elinor.

"Go on until I tell you to stop," he whispered, and poor frightened Mary Lou crept forward.

It was only a moment before a low "Stop!" brought her to a standstill, and the man lowered Rose Elinor so that the cousins stood side by side.

There were piles of pine-boughs heaped along one side of the cave; several rifles rested against the walls and there was a rough table at the far end. The little girls stood in the centre of the room not knowing what to do.

"Sit down!" commanded the man, and they sank down on the heap of pine-boughs, covered with a skin of soft fur, and looked fearfully up at their captor.

"No harm will come to you if you answer my questions and do exactly as I tell you," he said, in a more gentle voice.

Rose Elinor clasped Mary Lou's hand. She resolved that, no matter what the man said, she would keep a tight hold of her little cousin and defend her. While Mary Lou was at that moment saying to herself that she must think of some way to protect Rose Elinor,—

some way for them both to escape from this dreadful place and this man who looked at them so sternly.

The man drew a wooden stool directly in front of his captives and sat down.

"All I want is for you to tell me about your father and Jefferson," he said, endeavoring to speak in a friendly manner. "Now, I suppose you heard Jefferson say when our young friend Lafayette was expected to reach this part of Virginia?"

Both the little girls shook their heads, and the man's face clouded.

"Don't try any games with me, or it will be the worse for you," he said sternly. "If you do not tell me the truth, I mean to block up this cave and leave you here."

"Virginia young ladies always tell the truth," said Rose Elinor, and her dark eyes did not falter beneath the man's look, and at her cousin's words Mary Lou straightened her thin little figure and she, too, looked steadily at their captor.

"See that you remember that," growled the man. And now Rose Elinor quickly resolved that she would not tell the man a single word in regard to Mr. Jefferson, or of anything she had heard her father say in regard to the movements of the American troops. She now realized that this man was an enemy to America and that here was her chance to prove her own loyalty and courage. And she kept resolutely silent as the man continued to question her until he turned impatiently toward Mary Lou, whom he had not considered old enough to understand his questions.

"As your sister will not answer, you must," he said. But before he could continue Mary Lou, leaning closer to Rose Elinor as if to gain courage from her cousin's nearness, said:

"If you please, I am not her sister. I am the greatniece of Miss Pamela Fairfax Cutting, of Cutting Manor, and I only came to Rosecrest a few days since."

"What's that?" exclaimed the man, evidently greatly surprised, for the name of Miss Pamela Fairfax Cutting was well known to him as the name of a loyal supporter of the enemies of America.

"Are you an officer of Lord Cornwallis?" Mary Lou continued; "because my Great-aunt Pamela gave me a letter for Lord Cornwallis or one of his officers."

"I see, I see," muttered the man, who now believed that Miss Cutting had sent information to the British general by means of her little niece, and he was quick to notice that Rose Elinor was gazing at her cousin as if angry and amazed.

"A little Tory, after all my trouble!" he exclaimed. "And where is this letter?"

"It is in my trunk at Rosecrest and I am to give it only to Lord Cornwallis or one of his officers. Greataunt Pamela wrote that on the cover," said Mary Lou.

At this the man sprang to his feet.

"I'll find a way to get it! 'Twould well please his lordship if I bring him the letter. And, as Virginia young ladies never break a promise, you must promise to give it safely into my hands. Now I will lead you to the entrance of the cave when you have both made me a promise never to tell what has happened to you this morning. But, first of all, how am I to get the letter?"

"The letter is addressed to Lord Cornwallis, or to one of his officers," said Mary Lou steadily, "and, if you please, Great-aunt Pamela always told me that letters were to be given only to the person to whom they belonged."

The man's smile vanished and a puzzled frown appeared. He dared not threaten a niece of Miss Pamela Fairfax Cutting, but if he could secure the letter, that he doubted not contained valuable information, it would win him the approval of the great English general. He decided that he would find some way to get it without the knowledge of this stubborn little girl.

"Very well," he said quickly. "Do you want to leave this cave?"

"Yes! Oh, yes!" exclaimed Mary Lou eagerly, and Rose Elinor quickly echoed her words.

"Then promise that you will never try to find this cave; that you will never speak of your coming here, or tell anyone a word about me. If you do not promise this, I will block up the entrance to this cave and no one will ever discover you," and the man regarded the little girls with so fierce a look that their fears increased and they made the promise quickly.

Without another word the man led the way to the cave's entrance, pushed back the close growth of laurel bushes which so securely hid it, and said in a gruff whisper: "Back to the shore with you," and the two frightened little girls, stumbling in their eager haste, fled down the slope and ran swiftly along the shore until they were in sight of the boat.

"My lan'! Whare you bin? W'at yo' mean a dis'pe'rin' off de face ob de airth like yo' did?" screamed Clippy, as she came running toward the girls, closely followed by Jasper.

"You went to sleep, Clippy! You went to sleep!" said Rose Elinor. "We saw you fast asleep."

"Where is 'Lovely'?" Mary Lou demanded anxiously.

Clippy had entirely forgotten the dolls and when she returned to her former seat and picked up the unfortunate "Lovely," she discovered that the doll's face was cracked from forehead to chin.

Mary Lou held the doll carefully in her arms. She did not speak, for she feared she might cry. But "Lovely's" misfortunes only made her seem more dear to Mary Lou, and for the moment she entirely forgot the danger from which she and her cousin had just escaped.

Clippy watched the little girl anxiously, expecting to be well scolded for dropping the doll, but as Mary Lou remained silent Clippy turned toward her young mistress.

"Ef yo' ain' mos' starve den 'tis a wonder. De lunch am in de basket, an' yo' better step right up—Fer de lan' sakes! W'at yo' shut yo' eyes dat way for?" concluded the astonished Clippy. For Rose Elinor was standing directly in front of Clippy, her eyes tightly shut, as she whispered the words:

> " 'One—and—Two—and—Three,
> Witch, I am free!' "

CHAPTER X

AN ENEMY

THE four dolls were again on the carriage seat beside Clippy, while Mary Lou held "Lovely," whose poor face was in such a sad condition.

Now and then as they drove swiftly along toward Rosecrest, Mary Lou's glance rested on her cousin, but Rose Elinor seemed absorbed in her own thoughts and did not notice her. She was wondering what she ought to do about Mary Lou. If her cousin did indeed have a letter for Lord Cornwallis from Great-aunt Pamela, a letter that she had not mentioned until meeting a British soldier, as Rose Elinor was sure the man was who had taken them to the cave, why of course Mary Lou was a traitor and must no longer be cherished and trusted.

"I'll have to tell my father about that letter," thought Rose Elinor, "and if I do he will surely send Mary Lou straight back to Aunt Pamela," and now her glance rested on the thin little figure beside her. It did not seem really possible that anyone as small and frail, with such pleading blue eyes and so wistful a mouth as Mary Lou's could really be an enemy to her own country; and as Mary Lou's face brightened and the adoring smile that a look or word from Rose Elinor always brought to the little girl's face, Rose Elinor's heart softened. Perhaps, after all, Mary Lou did not have a letter to the British general, she thought hopefully. Perhaps Mary Lou had made up the story of a letter from Great-aunt Pamela to Lord Cornwallis so that the man would let them go, and Rose Elinor's face brightened at such a possibility, and she clasped her cousin's hand and whispered eagerly:

"You made up the story about the letter, didn't you, Mary Lou?"

Mary Lou's smile disappeared; she sat up a little straighter than usual and, for the first time in their acquaintance, Rose Elinor saw a little angry flush creep over her cousin's face as Mary Lou replied:

"I don't 'make up' stories, Rose Elinor. I have the letter, just as I told the man."

Clippy did not suppose the cousins' whispers were of any importance. "Lil' gals allers up ter som't'in'," she thought; neither was she surprised when Rose Elinor burst into angry tears.

"She bin mos' too good dese few days pas'," decided Clippy, making no effort to comfort her young mistress.

Mary Lou did not even look at her cousin, but drew farther into her own corner and turned her glance through the open window. She was nearly ready to cry herself at the thought that Rose Elinor believed her to have deliberately told an untruth.

Great-aunt Pamela had firmly impressed upon her small niece that there was no possible excuse for a lie, and that a person who stooped to lie at once ceased to be considered of any worth by honorable people. It did not occur to the little girl that Rose Elinor could think a "made-up story" a lesser fault than being the bearer of a letter between America's enemies. She felt that Rose Elinor must despise her or she could not have accused her of such a fault.

So both the little girls were troubled and unhappy on their arrival at Rosecrest, and Mrs. Moore wondered what had now happened to bring them home at so early an hour, and evidently after some disagreement.

Clippy shook her head hopelessly, in response to her mistress's questioning glance, and Mrs. Moore did not ask the girls what was troubling them. Rose Elinor, without a word to anyone, fled up-stairs and out to the platform on the roof, where she sank down on a broad cushioned seat.

"I must think what I will do about that letter," she told herself.

Mary Lou stood quietly on the porch steps until Clippy brought the dolls from the carriage. She held "Lovely" in such a way that the doll's bruised face was hidden against her shoulder, and when Mrs. Moore asked if she had enjoyed the excursion, she soberly responded:

"It was beautiful until we got to Gloucester Point and then it wasn't," and Mrs. Moore smiled in spite of her anxious thoughts.

"I will stay on the porch with the dolls, if you please," the little girl added, and Mrs. Moore promptly agreed, telling Clippy to bring a glass of cool milk for Miss Mary Lou; and then, satisfied that her young guest was well pleased to be left with the dolls for company, Mrs. Moore returned to the cool drawing-room.

As soon as Mary Lou was sure she was alone, she turned "Lovely's" head so that she could examine the doll's injured face and sighed deeply at the crack across the face, the scar of the missing nose and a scratch on the wax forehead. "Lovely" was the first doll Mary Lou had ever held in her arms; the first plaything she had ever owned, and it was a real grief to the little girl to have her first and dearest possession so injured.

"My cheek is nearly well," she thought, touching her own face where the beaded bag had struck her, "but your face stays hurt," and she looked down pityingly on the unlucky "Lovely."

"And everybody will think I have been very careless to let you get so knocked about," she whispered. "I'll just put some bandages over your poor face," and Mary Lou took the fine handkerchief from her pocket, tore it into strips, and carefully bandaged the doll's face. Then, having seated the other four dolls where no possible harm could befall them, she took "Lovely" and walked slowly down the rose-bordered walk to a small summer-house which was nearly hidden from the house by blossoming shrubs.

Although Mary Lou's first thoughts had been for "Lovely," the adventure at Gloucester Point still made her start at every sound, and when a clear, whistling call sounded from the thicket of shrubs she nearly dropped "Lovely," thinking it meant the approach of some enemy. But the call was so quickly followed by a clear trill and a gay song, that Mary Lou knew some woodland bird was near at hand, and she watched eagerly for a glimpse of the singer, and a moment later there was a flash of red from the undergrowth and the songster balanced himself on a rose-vine and cocked his crested red head as if to say:

"Here I am; notice my trim shape, and that I am not at all afraid of quiet people."

But Red-coat did not stay long to be admired. Mary Lou recognized him as a cardinal, many of whom nested near Great-aunt Pamela's, and the sight of this familiar bird brought her thoughts back to the letter safely hidden in her tin box, and to Rose Elinor's puzzling question regarding it. She recalled her cousin's saying that she hoped Mary Lou was a Tory, and poor Mary Lou began puzzling her little head over Rose Elinor's strange acts and words.

"She said, when I first came, that she had hoped I would be a Tory, and then when I said I was a Tory, before Mr. Jefferson cured me of it, Rose Elinor was angry, and to-day she seemed to hope I had told a made-up story and was angry when I said I had not! Oh, dear!" sighed the little girl. "I wish I knew what she meant," for it had not occurred to Mary Lou that Rose Elinor thought the possession of a letter to Lord Cornwallis meant that Mary Lou was a traitor.

But, while Mary Lou sat in the summer-house trying to account for her cousin's puzzling behavior, Rose Elinor lying on the broad, cushioned seat on the roof-top, had made up her mind what she must do about that mysterious letter. "I must take it from Mary Lou's box and give it to my father," she decided, "and not say a word to Mary Lou. After all, she is only nine years old, and probably she doesn't know that she ought not to be a messenger for America's enemies. It's Great-aunt Pamela Cutting's fault."

Before Rose Elinor had reached this conclusion she had several times closed her eyes tightly and repeated the "charm" that Mary Lou had told her. "I do believe it *is* a charm," she thought, as she sat up on the cushioned bench, her anger toward her cousin entirely forgotten, and looked idly out across the garden and driveway. As she looked an expression of terror came into her eyes. She slid from the bench and holding to the railing stared fixedly down at a skulking figure that, keeping close to sheltering shrubs and trees, was making its way toward the house.

"It's that man!" she whispered. "He is going into the rose-arbor! Oh-h!"

For as she looked the crawling figure had stood upright, stepped into the arbor and now reappeared holding Mary Lou in his arms, and ran swiftly along a side path and disappeared behind the tall trees that bordered the garden.

In an instant Rose Elinor was flying down the stairs screaming "Father! Father!" at the top of her voice. Mrs. Moore came running into the hallway just as Rose Elinor reached the lower stairs.

"Mary Lou! Mary Lou! That man has grabbed her and is carrying her away," screamed Rose Elinor, as she sped past her mother down the garden walk toward the rose-arbor.

For a moment Mrs. Moore believed that it was some sort of a game the girls were playing; nevertheless she ran after her little daughter, followed by two of the colored maids who had been sitting in the hall and had seen their young mistress and heard her frightened appeal.

Other servants came running through the house and into the garden, hurrying after Mrs. Moore and calling out that Miss Mary Lou had been carried off; and Mrs. Moore soon found herself surrounded by a chattering group, while Rose Elinor seemed to have vanished into space.

Mrs. Moore was not really alarmed about the little girls until a careful search of the garden failed to discover any trace of them. It was then late in the afternoon; Mr. Moore was in Williamsburg, ten miles distant, and would not return before evening, and she did not know what to do. It seemed impossible that Rose Elinor's declaration that a man had carried Mary Lou off could be true, but the little girl had vanished, Rose Elinor had disappeared in search of her and neither of them could be found; and when Mr. Moore reached Rosecrest at early twilight he found his wife almost too frightened to explain what had happened.

"Rose Elinor and Mary Lou have been kidnapped! Stolen right under my eyes," she declared, as she at last managed to tell the story of their mysterious disappearance.

Mr. Moore, followed by a number of servants, started down the driveway and turned toward Yorktown; there were several rough paths leading from the highway to the river and it was decided to search each of these in turn. Jasper had gone but a short distance along the first path when he heard a distant call. He stopped his horse and listened. In a moment he again heard "Help!" followed by a long call.

CHAPTER XI

THE CAVE-MAN

AFTER the man had freed Mary Lou and Rose Elinor and saw them running down the slope to the shore he instantly regretted his so doing.

"I ought to have made that yellow-haired girl promise to hand me over that letter to Cornwallis," he muttered. "If I could deliver such a message as that, his lordship would pay me handsomely." For this man was not a British soldier; he was a "hanger-on," always trying to evade danger, but carrying messages about the country from one English camp to another, and despised by both English and American soldiers.

He lurked about Gloucester Point until the little party had entered their boat and started for Yorktown; then, from a hiding-place in the underbrush, he pulled out a canoe and for a time keeping near the Gloucester shore, did not lose sight of them. Before the coach had left the "Swan" Tavern, he had landed at Yorktown and was running swiftly across the fields toward Rosecrest, and when Rose Elinor and Mary Lou stepped from the coach the man was lurking behind the rose-arbor.

He had resolved to hide until he could find a safe opportunity to seize the "yellow-headed little girl" and frighten her into a promise to give him the letter, and he called himself a fool for having let the two girls leave the cave without such a promise. This time he vowed to himself that he would have the letter or discover just how to secure it.

As he skulked near the arbor, startling the birds that nested in the shrubberies, he saw Mary Lou, carrying the dilapidated doll, come down the path. In a few minutes the little girl had seated herself near the arbor doorway, and the man smiled grimly to himself, sure that now his course was clear and that he would quickly receive either the letter itself or the little girl's promise to give it to him, and, with an ugly grin, he recalled Rose Elinor's assurance that "Virginia young ladies always keep a promise."

He slid through the arbor doorway so silently that he had lifted Mary Lou in his arms, with his big hand over her mouth, and was fleeing down a path toward the woodland before the little girl knew what had befallen her.

"The cave-man! And he is going to take me back to the cave!" thought the frightened child, clutching "Lovely" more tightly, as if to protect the doll from new misfortune.

Not until he reached the bank of the river, where his canoe lay safely under the shadow of overhanging laurel bushes, did the man speak, but now he whispered threateningly: "When I set you down you stand quietly. If you move or speak I will throw you into the river."

Mary Lou's blue eyes stared up at him pleadingly. She knew it would be no use to try to run away, and that no one could hear her calls. She stood silent and frightened near the laurels, until the man lifted her into the canoe, bidding her to sit quietly. Then with a firm stroke of his paddle he sent the light craft into the stream, and, before the search for Mary Lou had even begun, the little girl was again in the hillside cave.

As the man motioned her to a seat on the rough couch he said:

"You need not stay here a single moment longer than you wish. Just tell me that you will bring me that letter and I will carry you back to the garden as quickly as I took you away. Or, perhaps you have the letter in that deep pocket of yours? Or maybe it is hidden in that old doll you are hanging to! Ha! I believe it is!" he added, as Mary Lou took an even firmer clasp on her beloved "Lovely," and he wrenched the battered doll from Mary Lou's thin little hands and in a moment had torn off "Lovely's" muslin dress, twitched the bandage from the face, and finding himself mistaken and no letter concealed about the doll, he angrily flung it to the far end of the cave, exclaiming, "Tell me where that letter is?"

"I told you that it was safe in my trunk," Mary Lou managed to say.

The man did not have time to ask another question, for there was the sound of steps at the mouth of the cave and, in the light from the aperture in the roof, Mary Lou saw a figure coming toward them. Before the cave-man could even clutch at her dress she rushed past him and seized at the long cape that so nearly concealed the form of the newcomer.

"My doll! The cave-man has killed 'Lovely'!" she cried, and instantly a protecting arm was about the thin little shoulders and Mary Lou's fears vanished; she knew that she had found a friend.

"Well, Spoke? What's this child doing here?" questioned the visitor sharply. "I have no time to lose," he added.

"There is some trouble afoot at Yorktown. Men are riding down the highway, and, for all I know may be after me. Two boats are headed this way. Answer me quickly, for I must be off."

As the newcomer told of the boats leaving Yorktown the cave-man became greatly alarmed.

"They are coming here after me. That black-eyed girl has broken her promise and told of the cave," he said. "This girl has a letter for Cornwallis," he added quickly, "but we must get out of this. Those Yorktown men will shoot us without a word," and he fled toward the opening of the cave.

"Stop!" commanded the newcomer, and as his dark cape fell back from his shoulders, Mary Lou saw the gleam of his scarlet coat with its gold stripes, and knew that this handsome young man must be an officer of King George. "Did you kidnap this child?" he continued sharply, seizing Spoke's shoulder firmly.

"He grabbed me when I was in the rose-arbor, and he killed 'Lovely,'" exclaimed Mary Lou, before the cave-man could answer.

"You're a pretty fellow, aren't you!" exclaimed the young officer, shaking the man and pushing him aside. "Stand back! I will take this child to safety, and I hope the Yorktown men will discover you here. Don't let me ever find you near an English camp again. King George's men have no use for child-stealers," and lifting Mary Lou in his arms he strode past the slinking figure of the cave-man and stepped out on the slope, now shadowy in the gathering twilight.

A glance toward the river showed him that a well-filled boat was rapidly approaching the shore of Gloucester Point.

"Well, young miss, what is your name? Where do you live? And what about your letter for Lord Cornwallis?" he asked, smiling at the little girl, as if to reassure her.

Mary Lou answered him quickly. "I am Mary Lou Abbott, my father is an American soldier, and I live at Rosecrest. The letter to Lord Cornwallis, or to one of his officers, is from my Great-aunt Pamela."

The man nodded thoughtfully. He was used to making decisions quickly. To permit this boatload of American men to capture an English officer was not to be thought of. But they would surely be friends of this girl, and had come in search of her.

"Listen carefully, little maid," he said, setting Mary Lou on her own feet. "Go straight to the shore, and when your friends land tell them exactly what has happened. Describe the man who took you to the cave; tell your friends, with the compliments of Lieutenant Tarleton, of the British Legion, that I regret not to have the pleasure of meeting them, but hope to do so later on. And now good-bye and good luck," and drawing his cape about him the young officer disappeared in the thicket.

Mary Lou made her stumbling way to the shore, and it was her calls of "Here I am! Here I am," that guided Mr. Moore's boat, with Jasper at the helm, to the place where she stood. For Rose Elinor had promptly told her father of the morning's adventure at Gloucester Point; she had described the man and the cave, and had added that Mary Lou had told the man that she had a letter for Lord Cornwallis.

"And then he let us go. But I guess he came after the letter, and Mary Lou would not give it to him so he carried her off," Rose Elinor said, as her father anxiously questioned her.

And then suddenly Rose Elinor began to cry. "I promised never to tell a word about the man or the cave if he would let us go," she sobbed. "And now I have told!"

"Of course; just as you ought to do!" her father responded.

"To keep silent when you could rescue your cousin from great danger by speaking, would indeed be unforgivable. A promise made under such circumstances cannot be respected or kept. It has no value," he declared, and Rose Elinor's sobs ceased, and when Mr. Moore added that what she had told them might be the cause of finding Mary Lou and bringing her safely home within a few hours, she forgot the pain of the injured ankle and all the day's unhappiness, and smiled happily.

It was late that night when Mr. Moore and Mary Lou had reached Rosecrest, and Mammy Zella had lost no time in carrying the tired child to her room and putting her in bed. No search was made that night for the "cave-man," or for the cave. But the next day a party of men searched Gloucester Point, but without success.

Apparently Spoke had vanished, and the entrance to the cave could not be found.

Mr. Moore knew that Lieutenant Tarleton must have had some errand of importance in that vicinity, and it was only a few days later when news came that the Assembly at Charlottesville had been surprised by a party of English troops, commanded by Tarleton, that several members had been seized, and that Governor Jefferson had nearly been captured.

When this news came Rose Elinor was lying on a comfortable couch in her own pleasant chamber, the sprained ankle resting on a firm pillow. Mary Lou sat on a low footstool near the couch, and was busy making her cousin a necklace from the crystal beads in the brass box that the storekeeper had given them on that May day, which now seemed so far away.

Ever since the eventful day at Gloucester Point the two little cousins had hardly been separated for an hour. Mary Lou was eager to amuse and entertain Rose Elinor; she made up games, with the four dolls for actors; she sang queer old-fashioned songs that Great-aunt Pamela had taught her, greatly to Rose Elinor's delight, and she ran up and down-stairs many times each day to bring her cousin flowers from the garden, a special cake from the kitchen or to call Clippy for some service required by Rose Elinor. And each day Mary Lou seemed to gain in happiness. Her hands were not so much like little bird-claws, a little fullness came into her thin shoulders, and her cheeks began to show a healthy color. There was now only a tiny scar to show where the beaded bag had struck her, and Rose Elinor, who hoped earnestly that it might disappear, began to fear that the scar would always show on her cousin's cheek.

On this June day, as Mary Lou sat at work on the bead-necklace, Rose Elinor's glance rested on the scar and she said, almost as if talking to herself, "As long as that scar lasts I couldn't be angry at Mary Lou. I'd be afraid to."

"Then I hope it will never go away!" Mary Lou instantly responded, as she smiled happily at her cousin; the unfailing adoring smile that always gave Rose Elinor a little thrill of satisfaction and delight.

Just then Mr. Moore appeared in the doorway, a letter in one hand.

"I have some news of two of your friends, Mary Lou! Of Governor Jefferson, who discovered you when you were lost on the shores of Wormeley Creek, and of young Tarleton, the fine British officer, who rescued you from the cave-man. Not every young miss of your age can claim such important gentlemen for friends," he declared, smiling down at Mary Lou's eager face.

"Oh, Father! Sit down here by me and tell us your news," said Rose Elinor, and Mr. Moore seated himself beside his little daughter, unfolded the letter and began to read.

"'As for Tarleton, he must have ridden like the wind, with his well-mounted troops. The Virginia Legislature was in session, and but for Captain John Jouett, a resident on the route taken by Tarleton, and who suspected his object, mounted a swift horse, reached Charlottesville first and gave the alarm in time for most of the members to escape, the entire Legislature might have been captured.

"'As to Governor Jefferson,'" continued Mr. Moore, with a smiling nod at Mary Lou, "'he was entertaining guests when news came that Tarleton's troops were already coming up the road to Monticello, to Mr. Jefferson's house. There was no time to lose. Mr. Jefferson mounted his fleetest horse, and ten minutes later the British soldiers entered his house. But Governor Jefferson had escaped them.'"

"Oh!" exclaimed Rose Elinor. "To think of Mr. Jefferson being in danger!"

"It is indeed fortunate that he was warned in time," said Mr. Moore gravely, as he folded the letter.

CHAPTER XII

A DAY OF SURPRISES

THE June days passed quickly for the cousins, and early in July Rose Elinor's ankle had mended, and she was again able to climb up to the roof and enjoy the cool air and the pleasant views of the fields and the distant river.

During the days that she had been obliged to rest quietly in her own room the entire household, and the near-by neighbors as well, had done many friendly things to amuse the little girl.

Jasper had made her a pretty cane from a fine piece of hickory-wood; the handle was carved to resemble the leaves of a hickory-tree, and Mr. Moore praised the workmanship so admiringly that the delighted Jasper promptly began making another cane exactly like Rose Elinor's for his master.

Rose Elinor kept the cane close by her couch until she was able to hobble about, and long after her ankle had mended, she insisted on carrying the cane wherever she went.

Clippy made a bag of flowered chintz for her young mistress to hang on the arm of her couch. This bag had many pockets; a place for pencils and paper, for scissors, and a big pocket in which Rose Elinor could put "odds and ends," and it proved a useful and convenient gift.

Mammy Zella puzzled her head over new receipts for cakes, jellies and custards, and was so constantly in the kitchen that she and the cook, who was Mammy's younger sister, had many a wrangle over who should prepare dainties for Rose Elinor.

Mr. and Mrs. Nelson sent the little girl a parrot, thinking the bird's "conversation" would be sure to amuse her, and when "Cleopatra," as the parrot had been named, promptly exclaimed: "Down with the Tories," Rose laughed with delight, and never tired of the bird's somewhat limited vocabulary.

It was "Cleopatra" who had so frightened Mary Lou on her first visit to Nelson house, and she, too, was well pleased to have so accomplished a bird at Rosecrest.

But the gift that Rose Elinor prized most highly, and in which Mary Lou shared, came from Governor Thomas Jefferson. In spite of his many cares and great responsibilities he had not forgotten his young friends, and a few weeks after Tarleton's raid on Charlottesville, a messenger arrived at Rosecrest from Monticello, bringing two fat, woolly puppies; they were so exactly alike that had they not each worn a fine leather collar, with neat silver plates on which their names were engraved, it would have been nearly impossible to tell them apart.

One collar bore the name of "Lucky," and the other that of "Plucky." A note from Mr. Jefferson told the little cousins that they could arrange between themselves as to the dog they would choose.

"But it doesn't make any difference!" declared Rose Elinor.

It was finally decided, however, that "Lucky" should belong to Mary Lou, and "Plucky" should belong to Rose Elinor, and the little white dogs went bouncing about after their new owners like balls of white wool. They soon learned to answer to their names, and Mary Lou nearly forgot her grief over "Lovely's" sad fate in "Lucky's" faithful devotion.

But she did not entirely forget her unfortunate doll, and she sometimes reproached herself that she had not made some effort to rescue "Lovely" from the corner of the cave where the man had flung her.

The first day that Rose Elinor was able to go to the platform on the roof was a day of pleasant surprises for both the girls.

Mr. and Mrs. Moore had been making plans that it should be a day of delight for their little daughter. Rose Elinor had been unexpectedly patient and good-humored during the long summer days that she had been obliged to stay indoors, and, while her father and mother both realized that this pleasant fact was due largely to Mary Lou's devotion to her cousin, her eager willingness to stay beside Rose Elinor and do her best to entertain and amuse her, they felt, nevertheless, that Rose Elinor deserved some special notice should be taken of her recovery; and when Rose Elinor led the way to the roof, on an afternoon of early July, closely followed by Mary Lou, with Mr. and Mrs. Moore just behind them, and Mammy Zella and Clippy, both smiling and nodding to each other over their knowledge of the surprise in store for their young mistress, she had not imagined any special surprise had been planned for her.

As she reached the platform she was instantly surrounded by a group of girls about her own age, who laughed gaily over Rose Elinor's exclamations at the unexpected sight of her friends.

Two of the girls were the daughters of Mr. Page, who lived some miles away, and who had arrived just in time to reach the roof before Rose Elinor appeared. Then there was little Mary Carter, whose home was beyond Yorktown; and Frederica Greene, from Yorktown Village. These little girls had made occasional visits to Rosecrest, and Rose Elinor in turn had visited them. But since the invasion of Virginia by Cornwallis, there had been few interchanges of visits, and none of the young visitors had ever before seen Mary Lou.

As soon as Rose Elinor had welcomed her guests, she took Mary Lou by the hand and with her pretty smile said: "Mary Lou, these are my dearest friends," and carefully repeated their names, and then added,

"And Mary Lou is my dearest cousin and is going always to live at Rosecrest."

It was indeed a pretty sight on the broad platform on the roof of Rosecrest that July afternoon to see the group of girls in their dainty summer gowns, smiling and curtseying to Mary Lou, who, rosy-cheeked, happy and delighted over her cousin's recovery, seemed a very different child from the thin, sober-faced girl in the straight gray frock who had arrived in Miss Pamela Cutting's donkey-cart less than two months before at Rosecrest.

"Lucky" and "Plucky" promptly made their appearance and the visitors seemed greatly impressed to hear that the small dogs were a gift from Governor Thomas Jefferson, for even in 1781 he was considered a famous statesman, devoted to the welfare of America, and his name was beloved and venerated.

Luncheon was served on a round table, on the roof platform. There were ices in the shape of peaches and oranges; there was a round cake for each guest with her name on it in pink and white frosting. But before these appeared there were delicious fruit salads, served on crisp leaves of lettuce; sliced chicken and creamed potatoes, and small round biscuits, with heaped-up dishes of raspberries, and pitchers of cream.

After the little girls had feasted happily, Mrs. Moore suggested they should go to the garden. "I think your father has something to show you and Mary Lou," she said to Rose Elinor, as she led the way down the stairs to the front porch, the little girls all trooping behind her wondering if there was some new surprise in store for their little hostess.

"Whose pony-carriage is that?" asked Rose Elinor, thinking some other guests must have arrived, as she noticed a pair of black ponies, harnessed to a neat pony-cart, standing in the driveway. Jasper, in his finest livery, and beaming with smiles, stood at the ponies' heads.

Mrs. Moore made no response but went down the porch steps and the little girls all flocked after her.

"There seems to be a card tied to the whip," said Mrs. Moore. "You might look at it, Rose Elinor." And Rose Elinor darted forward, for she now felt sure she knew to whom those ponies and the fine cart belonged.

" 'This pair of ponies, "Sooty" and "Blacky," are the property of Miss Rose Elinor Moore and Miss Mary Lou Abbott,' " Rose Elinor read aloud; and instantly there was a chorus of exclamations as the girls all came near to read the card, to smooth the ponies' silky coats and to tell Rose Elinor and Mary Lou that the ponies could not be prettier.

Rose Elinor eagerly insisted that Mary Lou and Frederica Greene, who was the youngest girl of the party, should have the first ride in the new cart, and Mary Lou held the reins, while Jasper walked beside the ponies, who trotted down the driveway and back as if well pleased with their passengers.

Then Rose Elinor and Dolly Page took their turn; and Mollie Page and Mary Carter, being older than the other members of the party, had the last ride. But the girls all followed the ponies to the stable and watched Jasper unharness them.

"It's the finest present I could have—we could have, I mean," said Rose Elinor, slipping her hand under Mary Lou's arm as they turned to approach the house, and, seeing Mr. Moore coming toward the stables, the little girls ran to meet him.

"Dear Father, they are the splendidest present," Rose Elinor declared, clasping both hands about her father's arm.

"Splendidest!" echoed Mary Lou, skipping along beside her cousin. And Mr. Moore smiled as if he was as well pleased as the girls themselves.

It was early twilight when Jasper drove the big coach, with its four horses, to the porch, and the little visitors, all declaring it had been a lovely visit, said their good-byes to Mr. and Mrs. Moore and entered the coach, followed by Rose Elinor and Mary Lou, as the little cousins were to drive home with their guests as an ending to the day's pleasure.

As the big coach rolled down the driveway the girls' happy laughter floated back to Mr. and Mrs. Moore, who stood looking after it; and they smiled at each other at this proof that their plan to give their little daughter and her friends a day of complete happiness had been so successful.

The road was bordered by tall oaks, and from the undergrowth, where many woodland birds nested in safety, came the calls of the cardinal, the song sparrow and the thrush; and Dolly Page began a gay little song:

> "Betsy Bell and Mary Gray
>   They were two bonnie lasses;
>   They built a house beside a brae,
>   And roofed it o'er with rushes."

In a moment the other girls joined in the chorus of the old song that had been sung by Virginia's early settlers, and which was known and sung by every generation.

Jasper smiled and nodded approvingly. The girls' song sounded sweeter than the music of the birds to the faithful negro. He sent the four horses along at a good pace, as Mr. Moore had told him to be back at Rosecrest before dark.

Mr. Moore was on the porch, and as Mary Lou came up he put his arm about her and said:

"I have some good news for you, Mary Lou. Perhaps your father may soon be here."

Mary Lou's face instantly brightened; she forgot the ponies, and smiled so radiantly that both Rose Elinor and Mr. Moore smiled in response; but Mr. Moore hastened to warn the little girls that they must be careful not to mention the fact that Mary Lou's father was expected.

"He has been sent by General Washington with messages to Lafayette, who is now near Williamsburg, and when he has safely performed this errand he will come here for a few days. But his safety depends on keeping his visit a secret," said Mr. Moore, in so serious a voice that the girls instantly became grave, and promised not to let even Clippy hear them speak of Mr. Abbott and his hoped-for visit.

CHAPTER XIII

MARY LOU AND LIEUTENANT-COLONEL TARLETON

MARY LOU could now think only of her father's arrival. She awoke each morning with the hope that before the day ended he would come, and each night her last wish before sleep overtook her was that in the morning she would see her father.

For a time Rose Elinor had nearly forgotten her cousin's possession of the letter to the British general. She was so pleased with the ponies, the parrot and Plucky, her white dog, that her thoughts did not so constantly centre about the conflict that in these July days was constantly drawing nearer to Chesapeake Bay and to Yorktown itself.

It was only a few days after the surprise party, however, when the dangerous possibilities of the letter again entered her thoughts. She heard her father discussing the possible approach of Cornwallis's troops with a visiting neighbor, and heard him say that the possession of the Southern States was of the greatest importance to the English cause, as these States possessed rice, tobacco, indigo, and naval stores, more valuable to the army than what other States could furnish.

118

She heard the visitor declare that he believed Tories in the State were sending information to the British general, and at this Rose Elinor instantly remembered that Great-aunt Pamela Fairfax Cutting was a Tory, and that she had given Mary Lou a letter to Lord Cornwallis, and her former resolve to take the letter without her cousin's knowledge, so it could never reach its destination, again took possession of her thoughts. She no longer thought of Mary Lou as a possible Tory, but she had discovered that her little cousin always endeavored to keep a promise, and always told the exact truth.

"And so Mary Lou will think that she must not let anyone else have Great-aunt Pamela's letter, but that she must give it to Lord Cornwallis or one of his officers. But if it disappears from her trunk without Mary Lou knowing what became of it, why then the Tory general will never get it, and Mary Lou will not have been a Tory messenger," decided Rose Elinor, and resolved to secure this letter at the first opportunity. She wondered a little that her father had not spoken of it on the day of the girls' adventure at Gloucester Point, when she had told him of Mary Lou's declaration to the cave-man; but the fact was that Mr. Moore had not really understood what his little daughter had said.

Rose Elinor was not the only one who remembered the letter to Lord Cornwallis. The cave-man, in spite of

Lieutenant Tarleton's warning, was still lurking about Gloucester Point, and he still believed that if he could get possession of the letter of which the little yellow-haired girl had told him, that he would secure a reward on delivering it to Lord Cornwallis. Spoke had made several visits to Rosecrest, hoping for a chance to follow Mary Lou to her room and secure the coveted packet; and he might have been successful in this had it not been for the little white dogs, Lucky and Plucky, who were always close at the heels of their young owners, and whose sharp barks promptly gave notice of any intruder, so that Spoke had found it of no avail to hide behind hedges or to endeavor to creep into the house; Lucky and Plucky barked so fiercely, and bounded about like white woolly balls around his hiding-place, that on several occasions he had only time to reach the highway before servants were searching for intruders.

But nevertheless the man was resolved to get the letter; and Mary Lou could not imagine that the letter poor, mistaken Great-aunt Pamela had given her as a protection if British troops conquered American soldiers was to be a danger to her own safety and to that of Rosecrest.

Mary Lou's father arrived about the middle of July, but his little daughter was never told how he had reached Rosecrest. She awoke one morning to find a tall man in a faded uniform smiling down upon her, and knew instantly that it was her father. It was over a year since Captain Abbott had had a glimpse of his little daughter, and he was well pleased to see her rosy cheeks and to find her so happy and well cared for. She had so many things to tell him, and he was so glad to listen, that the morning hours fled very quickly.

"Your Aunt Pamela would give me up to the British, I suppose, if I tried to see her," Captain Abbott said laughingly, as he and Mary Lou sat together on the roof platform that sunny July morning.

"No, Father, I am sure she would not," Mary Lou responded eagerly; for the little girl was always quick to defend the crabbed old lady who, in spite of all her mistaken opinions, had really done the best she could for her homeless little niece.

"Well, I must not risk it. Indeed, I doubt if I should find her at Cutting Manor," said Captain Abbott, "for I hear that Cornwallis warned all his Tory friends to leave this vicinity, and I doubt not that Aunt Pamela is safe in some Tory stronghold."

This, indeed, proved to be the fact; for, when Yorktown was taken by the British in early August, Mr. Moore rode to Cutting Manor and discovered that Miss Cutting had removed to Richmond, intending to sail from there to England.

Captain Abbott's stay at Rosecrest was brief. He was to join Lafayette's army at Malvern Hill, and, on the second morning after his arrival, Mary Lou awoke to be told that her father was gone.

"But he is not far away, dear child, and you will see him again before many days," said Mrs. Moore, as Mary Lou's little face saddened and her blue eyes filled with tears. Rose Elinor stood close beside her little cousin and put her arm about Mary Lou, saying:

"You know your father said yesterday that you were to be brave when he was no longer here, and to remember that you were a little maid of Virginia."

Mary Lou nodded and choked back the tears. Just then Cleopatra called out, "Three cheers for Lafayette," which made both the little girls laugh. They had been endeavoring to teach this sentence to Cleopatra ever since her arrival at Rosecrest, and this was the first time the parrot had repeated the entire phrase. They both ran to praise and reward the bird, with Lucky and Plucky bounding after them. Then Rose Elinor suggested a visit to Blacky and Sooty, and when the girls reached the stables they decided it would be a fine morning for a drive. Jasper harnessed the ponies into the cart; the small dogs instantly jumped in, quite sure they were to be passengers, and the cousins took their seats. Rose Elinor held the reins, and as they drove off Jasper called after them:

"Don' go further on dan de bridge ober de creek, Missy Rose Elinor. I hears dat dar's queer fo'ks spyin' roun';" and Rose Elinor called back that she would turn at the bridge.

As the ponies turned from the drive into the highway they shied at something moving behind the hedge, and both the little white dogs began to bark; but neither of the girls imagined that it was anything more than a rabbit that caused the hedge to move and rustle.

But as soon as the pony-cart was well past the entrance, the cave-man lifted his head above the shrubbery and gazed after them.

"Good enough!" he whispered. "They and their confounded dogs are out of the way. Mr. Moore is on the roof of the house and Madame and the servants are busy. I'll find the trunk, and get the letter without much trouble;" and, crouching low, he made his way along the garden paths, keeping a sharp outlook lest someone should discover him. But he reached the house, crawled through an open window, and had reached the landing from which Mary Lou's chamber opened, before he heard any movement in the quiet house. Then suddenly a rough voice called:

"Down with all Tories! Down with all Tories!" And the man plunged down the stairs, ran out the front door and fled toward the woods, sure that he had been seen and was pursued. He did not stop until he was well out of sight of Rosecrest. If he had imagined that he had been defeated by a parrot he would doubtless have returned and ended Cleopatra's existence. But such a thought did not occur to him, as he fled through the woods seeking a secure hiding-place. Plunging at last into a thicket of laurel, he cowered panting with exhaustion and fright, sure that every noise of the woods was the footsteps of pursuers. But his fright did not make him relinquish his resolve to secure the letter.

In the meantime the ponies had reached the bridge over Wormeley Creek, and Rose Elinor was about to turn their heads toward Rosecrest, when Mary Lou exclaimed:

"Oh, Rose Elinor, there come soldiers on horseback!" For her quick glance had discovered a party of mounted horsemen coming rapidly down the turnpike that led to Williamsburg.

"They are English soldiers," declared Rose Elinor, noticing the red coats and fine horses of the soldiers who had now reached the bridge and were crossing in single file, and she quickly drew the ponies to one side of the road, intending to wait until the riders had passed.

There were six horsemen in the approaching party. On leaving the bridge, they again rode two abreast, and as the two in advance trotted near where the pony-carriage had halted, Mary Lou gave an exclamation of surprise, and the young officer nearest to the pony-carriage, who was mounted on a spirited bay horse, came to a sudden stop close beside the pony-cart.

"Why, here is the little maid of Gloucester Point Cave!" he said, smiling down at the astonished little girl.

Lieutenant-Colonel Tarleton was one of Cornwallis's most valued officers. He was a young man of great ability and courage; his dark, curling hair, his black eyes and friendly smile, together with the handsome uniform worn by the King's officers, made him a very attractive figure as he gracefully sat his fine horse and looked down at the two little girls in the pony-cart.

During the summer of 1781 this young officer headed many raids upon the towns and settlements of Virginia, capturing or destroying stores, and, when possible, taking American prisoners. At this moment of his encounter with Rose Elinor and Mary Lou he was on his way to take command of a detachment of soldiers near Williamsburg.

As Mary Lou recognized the friend who had rescued her from the cave-man her face beamed with delight.

"It's my soldier!" she declared, smiling up at him so radiantly that young Tarleton thought he had never before seen so charming a picture as the yellow-haired little girl, holding a small, round white dog that was vainly endeavoring to escape her grasp and attack the red-coated soldier.

"Rose Elinor! Rose Elinor! This is the soldier who found me in the cave and told me what to do," said Mary Lou eagerly, fully expecting her cousin to be as pleased as she was herself at so happy a meeting.

But Rose Elinor's eyes were fixed straight ahead. After one scornful glance at the redcoats she had not again looked at them; and, as Mary Lou spoke, she suddenly brought her whip down across the ponies, who sprang forward and dashed on to the bridge, leaving the young officer gazing after them in amazement.

His companions laughed as he swung his horse back to the road.

"A young American holding the reins, eh?" questioned one of the officers as they all trotted on together.

Tarleton nodded, ill-pleased that he could not have questioned the little girls, or, at least, have left them in a more friendly manner. But he had no time to ride after them, and, in spite of his former success and his undoubted courage, he knew that Lafayette's soldiers were on the alert for his capture and that it was not safe to linger; especially if the dark-eyed girl who had sent the ponies plunging across the bridge meant to inform her friends that Lieutenant-Colonel Tarleton was riding down the highway.

So the party of British soldiers turned toward Williamsburg, riding at their swiftest pace; and long before the cousins reached Rosecrest Tarleton was safe in a British encampment.

Mary Lou had been too much startled and astonished to speak as the ponies darted off. She had, indeed, nearly tumbled from her seat at the unexpected start; and, clutching Lucky with one hand, while she grasped the seat rail with the other, she sat silent and wondering until the ponies' pace changed from a plunging gallop to a moderate trot; then, looking firmly at her cousin, Mary Lou said steadily:

"I s'pose you wish that the English officer had left me in the cave."

"I forgot that the English soldier rescued you from the cave; truly I did, Mary Lou. All I remembered was that he was the man who tried to capture Mr. Thomas Jefferson," and Rose Elinor turned a pleading glance toward her little cousin; and as she looked, a smile crept over her face, for Mary Lou's eyes were tightly closed and Rose Elinor heard a faint voice whispering:

"'One—and—Two—and—Three!'"

CHAPTER XIV

AN UNEXPECTED VISITOR

LONG before the ponies reached Rosecrest the little cousins were again the best of friends; for Mary Lou was quite ready to believe that her adored cousin could not willingly be impolite, even to the enemies of her country; and she was rather ashamed of her own angry impatience, while Rose Elinor, in her turn, had been well pleased to see Mary Lou try the "charm" against ill-temper, in which the elder girl now really believed; and she had handsomely declared herself to blame for starting the ponies before Mary Lou could thank Lieutenant Tarleton for rescuing her from the cave.

Jasper met the little girls on the driveway to the house.

"Yo' jump out right h'ar," he said soberly, "an' go up to de house as quiet as yo' can. Massa Moore got com'ny on de po'ch, an' don' wan' ter be 'sturbed."

The little girls promptly obeyed, and, taking one of the garden paths, made their way to the house and entered through a side door. Clippy was on the outlook for them, but her face was so sober that Rose Elinor wondered what had happened. Before she could ask any questions, however, Clippy whispered:

"Who yo' s'pose is a-settin' on de po'ch dis minit?" and before either of the little girls could speak, she answered her own question:

"It's de young Frenchman, Laffyit! He be a-sittin' an' a-talkin' as if he wa'n't no better dan odder fo'ks; an' as if he wa'n't skeered o' no-buddy."

"Oh, Clippy! Couldn't we see him?" whispered Rose Elinor eagerly; for there was not a child in Virginia who did not long to see the young hero who had come across the seas to aid Americans in their struggle against oppression.

Clippy shook her head firmly. "Yo' pa say no libin' pusson is to step on dat po'ch! An' dar's two sojers in de hall, an' a' army hid roun' de house!" And Clippy rolled her eyes and raised both hands, endeavoring to impress the little girls with the importance of the occasion.

"But could we not just lean out of the door and see him?" pleaded Mary Lou.

Clippy hesitated. She was very well pleased to have the power to grant such an important favor, and finally consented to permit the little girls to tiptoe carefully down the hall and take one look through the open doorway.

"Jes' one look, yo' 'member. An' if yo' sees him, or if yo' don' sees him, yo' ain' ter look twict!" she warned them. "An' I'll jes' take dose lille dogs," she added; and Rose Elinor and Mary Lou promptly handed over

Lucky and Plucky, who were none too well pleased to be promptly shut in a small room at the rear of the house.

Hand in hand the cousins tiptoed noiselessly down the long hall. At the foot of the stairway stood two American soldiers on guard; for the young Frenchman took as few chances of surprise as possible. The soldiers smiled and nodded as the eager-faced girls stole noiselessly toward the door; but just before they reached it they both stopped suddenly, and standing hand-in-hand made their best curtsey, for Lafayette had risen and was facing the doorway only a few steps from the awestricken little girls.

"*Ah! les jeune demoiselles!*" said the smiling young man, bowing low in response to the girls' curtsies, and the cousins looked up, a little fearfully, to find his kindly look resting upon them.

"My little daughter, Rose Elinor, and her cousin, Mary Lou Abbott," said Mr. Moore, well pleased that the girls should have the honor of meeting the distinguished soldier. And as he spoke their names the girls curtseyed again, and then stepped a little back as the young Frenchman and Mr. Moore entered the hall and made their way to a rear entrance, followed by the two soldiers.

In a few moments there sounded the noise of horses' feet, and when Mr. Moore returned to the hall he found the two little girls with clasped hands stand-ing gazing at the doorway through which Lafayette had vanished.

"He's off!" declared Mr. Moore. "And heaven grant that Tarleton's raiders be not in this vicinity!"

"Oh! They are! Six of them!" declared Mary Lou; and, both talking at once, the little girls told the story of meeting the six British soldiers at the bridge.

Mr. Moore's face grew very serious as he heard that Tarleton and his men had been so near Rosecrest. All during July, 1781, Lafayette had hovered about Corn-wallis, shifting his camp almost daily. As yet they had not come to open warfare. Lafayette had made this visit to Rosecrest to secure news from Governor Jef-ferson in regard to supplies and reinforcements, and it was indeed fortunate that he did not encounter Tar-leton. Mr. Moore could only hope the British officer and his men would not discover Lafayette's vicinity, as they fortunately did not.

The vanguard of Lafayette's army was, in mid-July, 1781, at the time of his call upon Mr. Moore, within twelve miles of Williamsburg, and Lord Cornwallis was none too well pleased with its neighborhood. Men who had given the English general reason to fear them were in it: General Campbell, who took a little army from him at King's Mountain, and General Morgan, who took another at Cowpens.

And so Cornwallis was hastening to his fate at York-town, and Lafayette awaited the British general's next move.

Rose Elinor had been far more impressed by Lafayette's visit, and by the fact that she had really seen and spoken to the young Frenchman, than her cousin had been, and for the remainder of the day she was very quiet and thoughtful. She heard her father say that if Lafayette could only discover in which direction Cornwallis intended to move it might be possible to defeat him; and Rose Elinor thought what a wonderful and splendid thing it would be if she, a little maid of Virginia, could be the one to carry such information to him. Her thoughts centered upon the letter to Cornwallis. It might contain some word that would help the American army; and, as this possibility occurred to her, Rose Elinor made up her mind that she would secure the letter that very night and find a way to deliver it to Lafayette.

Mary Lou's thoughts, however, did not linger about Lafayette as much as upon the English officer. If Rose Elinor had only given her a chance to again thank him, thought Mary Lou, and, perhaps, to ask him if he had noticed a broken doll in the corner of the cave at Gloucester Point, for the little girl could not really give up the hope that in some way she might rescue "Lovely." So both the girls were unusually quiet at supper; but Mr. and Mrs. Moore did not think this at all to be wondered at. It had surely been an eventful day for the little cousins; a meeting with Tarleton and his raiders, followed by a sight of the Marquis de Lafayette, might well impress them; and when, at an earlier hour than usual, the little girls said good-night and retired to their chambers, no one was surprised except Mammy Zella, who followed Rose Elinor and helped her prepare for bed with a vague suspicion that "Miss Rose Elinor she be a-conjurin' up' som' mis-ch'ef; she sho' be!" And Mammy resolved to sleep that night "wid one ear wide open," in case her young mistress should attempt mischief before morning.

Fortunately for Rose Elinor's plans, however, Mammy Zella was a good sleeper, and when the soft darkness of the midsummer night had settled over Rosecrest she had fallen into a deep slumber from which she did not awaken until aroused at midnight by the screams of her young mistress.

Rose Elinor lay quietly in bed waiting until the house was still. The big clock in the hall struck twelve; Rose Elinor counted every stroke, and, as the final one echoed along the corridors, she sat up in bed, peered for a moment about the shadowy room, and then her feet touched the floor, and she moved noiselessly to the door. Her cousin's chamber was just across the hallway, and both the doors were wide open. A little breeze, filled with the fragrance of the honeysuckle, drifted in through the windows; the note of a night-loving bird rose musically from the big oak-tree near the house; and as Rose Elinor stood in the doorway of her cousin's room, she thought to herself that, after all, it was a very easy and pleasant errand to secure the letter, and smiled at the remembrance of her fear of leaving her own room at night.

But at that very moment of her sense of security and success she saw a dark shadow at the western window of her cousin's room, and held her breath in fear. First the head and shoulders of a man pushed between the muslin curtains, and in a moment the tall figure of the cave-man stood close to the wall, while his eyes endeavored to become familiar with the room and to discover the location of the trunk.

Rose Elinor instantly believed that Spoke had come to carry her cousin away, and at this thought she forgot her terror and ran toward Mary Lou's bed, screaming at the top of her voice, "The cave-man! Mary Lou! The cave-man!"

Rose Elinor's screams awakened Cleopatra, who promptly began to shriek. In an instant Mammy Zella came stumbling into the room and added her voice to the tumult. Lucky and Plucky, who, for the first time, had been left down-stairs in the small room where Clippy had shut them in, were heard barking fiercely, and the whole house was in an uproar when the trembling Spoke managed to slide through the window, lower himself by the stout vines that grew against the outer wall, and reach the driveway.

A pistol shot rang out after the fleeing figure, as Mr. Moore darted from the house in pursuit of the man; but Spoke had disappeared, and it was plainly of no avail to search for him in the darkness.

Mr. Moore declared that Rose Elinor was a little heroine to have fled to her cousin's rescue; for he took it quite for granted that, at some noise in Mary Lou's room, his little daughter had awakened and, without thought for her own safety, had hastened to the aid of her cousin.

Rose Elinor's face flushed beneath his praise. She knew that she did not deserve it, but she dared not tell her father that she had been creeping into Mary Lou's room to take a letter from her cousin's trunk.

But as she stood silent, she was suddenly astonished to hear Mary Lou calmly announce:

"I guess the cave-man was after Great-aunt Pamela's letter to Cornwallis."

"To Cornwallis? Why, what do you mean?" questioned Mr. Moore, utterly amazed at his little cousin's words.

"Don't you remember? I told you about it after that day at Gloucester Point," said Mary Lou.

Mr. Moore shook his head. He had no recollection of it. "I had better take charge of it for you," he suggested; and at this Mary Lou's face became very grave.

"It says on the package that I am to give it only to 'Lord Cornwallis or to one of his officers,' so, of course, I cannot give it to you," responded Mary Lou, while Mr. Moore looked even more surprised at her response than he had at her first announcement.

"But you can read the address yourself," the little girl added, running across the room and opening the small trunk, from which she took the packet and handed it to him.

As Mr. Moore read the inscription: " 'To Lieutenant-General Earl Cornwallis—or to any officer in the service of King George,'" and then the words that Miss Cutting had written to Mary Lou, saying that, in time of danger, the letter would secure her protection, his face brightened, and he returned the packet to Mary Lou with a smile, saying, "Very well, my dear, you may keep the letter."

IN A MOMENT THE LETTER WAS IN HER HAND

CHAPTER XV

THE LETTER

THE cave-man, after this midnight effort to get possession of the packet for Cornwallis, decided that he must think of some other way than entering Rosecrest, and it now occurred to him that if Cornwallis was to know of the existence of such a letter he would reward whoever brought the news and would promptly take measures to obtain it.

"I ought to have thought of that plan long ago," muttered Spoke, and at once started out for the English camp near Williamsburg, confident that he would be well rewarded for the information that a "little yellow-haired girl" visiting at Rosecrest, near the York River, had in her possession a letter addressed to Lord Cornwallis.

"I reckon the English general 'll know just how to get that letter. He'll send soldiers after it; maybe make me an officer for fetching the news," Spoke hopefully muttered to himself as he hastened across fields and through woodlands to the distant camp.

And he was right in thinking that Lord Cornwallis would wish to know the contents of any letter addressed to him; and as soon as Spoke reached the camp, where he was known to several of the officers, he was promptly admitted to the presence of Cornwallis.

Earl Charles Cornwallis, Lieutenant-General in the British Army, was at that time second in command of the King's forces in America. He made his first appearance in the field in 1776, and had now been sent to conquer the Southern States. He was never lacking in resources, and although cold and severe in manner, he was trusted and beloved by his soldiers.

Lord Cornwallis's glance seemed to read the mind of Spoke instantly; for, as the man finished his story of the letter now in the possession of Mary Lou, the British general nodded coldly.

"Very well. I shall be riding in the direction of Yorktown shortly and will call at Rosecrest for the letter. If it be of any value to the King's army you will hear from me again. In the meantime," and he drew a gold piece from his pocket and pushed it across the rough table toward his visitor, "this will pay you for your trouble."

Spoke picked up the coin and silently left the room. He was angry and disappointed at the reception of his news, and now began to doubt if, after all, the letter was of any importance. But he did not dare show his anger, and slunk away from the camp.

Rose Elinor's opportunity to secure the letter came one morning in early August. Mary Lou was in the garden, and Rose Elinor went straight to her cousin's chamber, opened the trunk, and in a moment the letter to Cornwallis was in her hand. She slipped it into the deep pocket of her muslin skirt and ran across the hallway to her own room, where she put on her broadbrimmed hat of white straw, and then, carefully avoiding any chance of being seen by the servants, she made her way to the rear of the house and reached the stable without having attracted the attention of anyone.

Jasper was that morning driving Mr. and Mrs. Moore to the house of a neighbor, where they were to spend the day, and it was this fact that had made Rose Elinor determine that the time had come to carry out her plan of delivering the letter into the hands of Lafayette.

The stables were quiet and deserted; for the boy who helped Jasper had decided on a day's vacation and disappeared. Blacky and Sooty stood in their stalls as if expecting their young mistress, and Rose Elinor hesitated only for a moment as to the pony she should choose to carry her on the ride to find Lafayette.

"Sooty!" she said aloud, and then looked quickly about, fearful that she might have been heard. But only the sound of Sooty's feet, as she led him from his stall, broke the stillness of the big stable.

Rose Elinor slipped a bridle over the pony's head and then folded a blanket and firmly strapped it over his back. She had never ridden horseback, but she had no doubt that she could balance herself on Sooty's fat back and ride without difficulty. She did not mount in the stable, but led the pony through a rear door into a field, where, keeping behind hedges, she finally reached a path that led directly to the bridge over Wormeley Creek, and mounting Sooty, she urged the pony forward at his best speed. Rose Elinor, that very morning, had heard her father describe the location of Lafayette's camp, and she was confident that she could reach it and return home before her father and mother were back from their visit. With Mary Lou absorbed in her storybook and the servants all busy with their work, she felt sure she would not be missed until the hour for luncheon. "And soon after that I will be home," she thought.

It was several days since Sooty had enjoyed a good gallop, and he darted forward along the path so swiftly that at first Rose Elinor found it difficult to keep her seat, but as she turned him into a broad road the pony's pace lessened and he trotted along so evenly that his rider began to look about her and to enjoy her ride. She had no doubt that she was about to render a great service to the American Army, and was sure that, even if her father did not think a letter from Great-aunt Pamela to the British general of any importance, Lafayette would consider such a letter valuable.

"Perhaps he may even ride back with me and tell my father that this letter has given him important news," thought Rose Elinor hopefully.

She knew exactly the direction to take, and, thanks to Sooty's speed and excellent behavior, she came within hail of the leafy shelters of the troops of Lafayette well before the hour of noon. A young soldier stepped out on the pathway and brought Sooty to a sudden halt, and Rose Elinor slid off the pony's back with a little sigh of relief.

"I'm dreadfully tired," she announced, adding, before the surprised soldier could speak, "I have come to see General Lafayette."

"You don't tell me! Well, I guess the General will have something to say about that," responded the youth, a broad grin spreading over his sunburnt face. "You step along with me. *If* you please!" and he bowed so low that he nearly lost his balance, and Rose Elinor looked at him reprovingly; but she followed on behind him as he led Sooty toward the entrance of a large wigwam that the soldiers had erected as a shield from the rays of the midsummer heat.

At the entrance of the wigwam a number of soldiers were lounging, but at the sight of the newcomer they sprang to their feet.

"This young lady is a Princess of Virginia who has come to present this black charger to General Lafayette," announced the grinning youth, again bowing low to Rose Elinor. But Rose Elinor was not at all abashed by his endeavor to make fun of her. She had been quick to notice a figure sitting just inside the entrance to the wigwam, and, without a glance at the youth, who still held Sooty's bridle rein, she stepped past the group of loungers and, curtseying in the doorway of the wigwam, announced:

"If you please, I am Miss Rose Elinor Moore, of Rosecrest, and I wish to speak with General Lafayette, who is a friend of my father's."

She could have said nothing that would have so quickly gained her the attention she desired. The grinning youth instantly became serious and a little alarmed. He handed Sooty's bridle-rein to the man nearest him and promptly vanished, before the officer to whom Rose Elinor had addressed herself had stepped from the shelter and stood smiling down at this unexpected visitor.

"I am sure the General will be delighted to see you, Miss Rose Elinor Moore. If you will step into this poor shelter and be seated, I will inform him of your arrival," he responded, with what, Rose Elinor felt, was exactly the proper manner, and, curtseying again, she entered the wigwam and sat down on a rough stool that stood near the door.

In a few moments the officer returned.

"General Lafayette will be pleased if you will kindly accompany me to his presence," he said gravely.

As Rose Elinor left the wigwam and walked along beside the officer, she looked about, hoping the grinning boy who had tried to make fun of her might see that his betters considered her a person of importance; but the youth was not to be seen, nor did he again show himself while Rose Elinor remained in camp.

The young French general received his little visitor with great kindness. Before she could tell her errand he insisted that she should share his luncheon, which was just being served on a table at the entrance of his tent. Rose Elinor was hungry and thirsty, but as she took her seat opposite the great Lafayette, whom the British general called "a mere boy," she forgot her hunger and fatigue and thought only of the great honor that had befallen her.

It was a very plain and simple luncheon, not nearly as good as was daily set before Rose Elinor in her own home, but she never forgot the food she tasted that day or the worn face of the young general who, in the midst of his great responsibilities and anxieties, took time to be polite and kind to a little girl.

When luncheon was over, and Rose Elinor had answered Lafayette's inquiries about her family, he said, "You have, perhaps, some message for me?"

Rose Elinor flushed happily as she drew the sealed packet from her pocket and handed it to Lafayette.

"My Great-aunt Pamela is a Tory, and she wrote this letter and gave it to Mary Lou," she explained eagerly.

For a moment, after reading the inscription on the letter, Lafayette balanced it in his hand, his face grave and thoughtful. "And you thought it might contain some information that would be of value to me?" he said questioningly. "I thank you, little maid. As this letter commends your cousin to the care of Lord Cornwallis, I think, and I am sure you agree, that I must make certain she does not need protection from him."

Rose Elinor smiled in agreement, and waited patiently while Lafayette stepped to a table in the rear of the tent, where he seated himself, wrote a few words, and quickly returned to his little visitor with a freshly sealed and folded packet.

"Take this to your little cousin," he said, smiling gravely. "And if, by any ill fortune, she should require to ask help from English troops, tell her to open this, and to obey the instructions." And Lafayette handed Rose Elinor the packet, which she promptly slipped into her pocket. The officer who had brought her to the General's tent now appeared leading Sooty, and Rose Elinor realized that the time had come to take leave of the young Frenchman.

"Perhaps we may soon meet again, and, until we do, it will be wiser not to mention the letter you brought me," he said.

Rose Elinor agreed eagerly; the general bade her a kindly good-bye; the officer lifted her to the pony's back and walked beside her until they were some distance from camp, then he left her with a smiling bow, and Rose Elinor found herself homeward bound.

She felt well pleased with the success of her errand, and thrilled at the thought that her pocket held a letter, as she believed, from the French general. She did not for many weeks discover that Lafayette, with his high sense of personal honor, had not opened the letter of Miss Pamela Cutting to the British general; he had only enclosed it in another wrapper and written upon it: "To be opened by Miss Mary Lou Abbott when she meets Lord Cornwallis."

In this manner he had avoided hurting the feelings of Rose Elinor, who had wished to be of assistance to the cause for which the young Frenchman was fighting.

It was late in the afternoon when Rose Elinor reached Rosecrest, and she rode straight to the stables, wondering what Jasper would say when he saw she tired pony.

But Jasper was not there, nor were the big coach-horses in their stalls.

Then the little girl slowly made her way to the house, expecting at every step to see Mammy Zella or Clippy running toward her or to hear Mary Lou calling her name. But she entered the house without seeing anyone; and when, standing in the hall, she called "Clippy! Clippy!" there was no response.

CHAPTER XVI

MARY LOU VISITS CORNWALLIS

IN a moment, however, Plucky's welcoming bark sounded from an upper floor, and the little white dog, closely followed by Lucky and Mary Lou, came bounding down the stairs. Before Rose Elinor could speak Mary Lou exclaimed:

"Hurry! Hurry! Rose Elinor, where have you been? Come quick! Come!" and Mary Lou seized her cousin by the arm and drew her toward the stairway.

"What is it?" Rose Elinor asked, wondering what could have happened to make Mary Lou forgetful that they had been separated for hours, and noticing that her little cousin was evidently greatly excited.

"We can see them from the roof. Hurry!" urged Mary Lou. But Rose Elinor did not move. She began to feel puzzled and angry, but the little white scar showed more distinctly than usual on Mary Lou's flushed cheek, and Rose Elinor kept control of her impulsive temper and followed her cousin up to the platform on the roof, where she found Clippy and Mammy Zella, as well as the cook and housemaid, gathered in a group near the railing.

147

"Whar on earth you bin?" began Mammy Zella, turning an accusing glance toward Rose Elinor, but the next instant pointing to the glimpse of distant highway leading toward Yorktown from Williamsburg.

"Look dar! Dar's de King's army a-marchin' straight in to Yorkto'n. An' de Lawd only knows what's happen' to yo' pa and ma!"

Rose Elinor ran to the railing and looked eagerly toward the far-off slope. Mammy Zella was right. She could see the well-mounted troops of the British Army, the sunlight of the late afternoon reflected on the glistening brass and silver of their accoutrements, and bringing out the bright scarlet of their uniforms, as platoon after platoon moved steadily along, vanishing where the road curved toward the coast.

"Dar's t'ousan's an' t'ousan's ob 'em!" declared Clippy, staring with frightened eyes at her young mistress.

But Rose Elinor did not hear her. Her thoughts flew back to the young French officer in command of the American Army, and she wondered if his troops would not soon follow those of the English general.

Except for the exclamations of Clippy no one spoke until the last of the marching troops had disappeared, and then Mammy Zella promptly took command of the situation.

"H'ar, yo' Essie! We's gotter eat, ain' we? What Mistress Moore gwine ter say w'en dar ain' no food in de house?" and she glared fiercely at the frightened cook, who, declaring that Rosecrest would be burned before morning, hurried off to the kitchen, followed by the housemaid. Clippy also disappeared, and Mammy Zella was about to again question her young mistress as to where she had been during the day, when Mrs. Moore came up the stairway to the platform.

Her face was pale, and it was evident that she was greatly fatigued, but she showed no signs of fright as she greeted the little girls; nor did she, for the moment, speak of what had befallen her a few hours before, when a troop of Cornwallis's men had stopped the coach, ordered the frightened Jasper to unharness the horses, which they had at once driven off, and left Mrs. Moore and her coachman to reach home as best they could. It was a walk of six miles, and, as they had not dared keep to the highway, they had made their way across fields and through woods.

On their arrival that morning at Colonel Carter's Mr. Moore was told that Governor Jefferson required his presence at Charlottesville, and, with a number of other gentlemen of the neighborhood, he had started at once, not imagining his family were in any danger from the approach of the enemy. But now the British force, in the early days of August, 1781, suddenly made its appearance at Yorktown, on the Virginia peninsula, a spot Cornwallis was to leave as a prisoner of war.

But the little household at Rosecrest, on that August afternoon, were too surprised and alarmed to look forward to the defeat of Cornwallis. Mrs. Moore did her best to quiet and reassure the servants, and said nothing that would alarm Rose Elinor or Mary Lou; but both the little girls, nevertheless, realized that the presence of the enemy's troops at Yorktown was a menace to the safety of Rosecrest. That night Mrs. Moore had the little girls sleep in her chamber, and Lucky and Plucky also, while Mammy Zella brought her bed to the upper hall, and insisted on being allowed to sleep just outside their door.

Rose Elinor was so tired by her day's excursion that she did not waken until morning, and her first thought was that the packet Lafayette had given her was still in the deep pocket of her muslin dress. "I'll put it in Mary Lou's trunk the moment I get up," she resolved, wondering why the house seemed so unusually quiet.

Mary Lou was fast asleep, and Mrs. Moore was not in the room; so Rose Elinor slid out of bed, drew out the packet from the pocket of the dress she had worn on the previous day, and ran down the hall to her cousin's chamber. It took but a few moments to slip the packet into the small trunk and return to her mother's room, where she found Mammy Zella gazing at her empty bed with evident alarm.

"Miss Rose Elinor, don' yo' wander off ag'in de way yo' did yesserday. 'Tain' safe! An' wot yo' t'ink,

Missy! Dat Essie an' dat odder misserbul gal hab put off an' lef' us!"

Essie and "de odder misserbul gal" were not the only people in the vicinity of Yorktown who promptly disappeared during the first days of August, 1781; and as the weeks passed it became impossible for many loyal people to stay in their homes. Raiders from the British camp drove off the cattle, stripped the fields of the growing crops, and took possession of anything that would add to the well-being of officers and soldiers.

For the first time in her life Rose Elinor dressed herself that morning without any assistance, except what Mary Lou eagerly offered, for Mammy Zella and Jasper were now the only servants left in or about the big mansion.

Rose Elinor's visit to Lafayette still remained a secret; in fact the little girl herself had nearly forgotten it in the trouble and excitement that had so quickly followed that day. She and Mary Lou were so busy that neither of them found any time to play with dolls, or to wander about the garden with Lucky and Plucky. After the raid on the barns and stables, Jasper had turned the black ponies, which the British soldiers evidently had not considered worth taking, into a pasture beyond the barns, and the cousins did not see Blacky and Sooty for several weeks.

Mary Lou was perhaps happier than she had ever been. She could do so many useful things, that not a day passed when Mrs. Moore did not praise her, and often declared that she did not know what she would do without her. Rose Elinor was always exclaiming in delight over her cousin's ability to set a table, mend a torn garment or make a bed; so that the little girl began to feel herself really of importance, and enjoyed the work more, even, than the long days when she had only played with dolls or drove about behind Blacky and Sooty.

She was so busy and happy that she did not realize that, only a few miles away, the British army were encamped, and that those she loved best were in danger. But one day she opened her trunk to take out an apron that she remembered Great-aunt Pamela had put in, and the little white packet lay before her.

Mary Lou held it in both hands, but she did not read the new inscription. She remembered that this was to be given to Lord Cornwallis if she ever needed protection, and suddenly Mary Lou comprehended that this letter had been given her to use at just such a time as now confronted her. She recalled Mammy Zella's fear: "'Dat ole Cornwallis may burn dis house or, maybe, send his sogers to lib har.'" And she knew that Mrs. Moore feared a possible return of the raiders who had driven off her stock.

Sitting there before the open trunk with the packet in her hand, Mary Lou felt that she was to blame for the daily hardships of Rose Elinor and Mrs. Moore.

"I ought to have carried this letter to Lord Cornwallis the very day he came to Yorktown. Oh dear!" and she sniffed sorrowfully. But in a moment she had resolved that no more time was to be lost; she would start at once for Yorktown, deliver the letter to Lord Cornwallis, and then hurry back and tell Mrs. Moore and Rose Elinor what she had done, and that the British general would not permit his soldiers to cause them any further trouble.

The thought that at last she could do a real service for the cousins who had been so kind to her made Mary Lou very happy. Perhaps, she thought happily, Lord Cornwallis would send back all the things he had taken from Rosecrest, and Mr. Moore be allowed to return in safety. The little girl's thoughts were full of hopeful possibilities as she tied on her pretty straw hat, put the packet in a silk bag that Rose Elinor had given her, and without a word to anyone in regard to her destination or errand, she went down the broad stairway to the garden and turned toward the highway, with Lucky trotting beside her.

Mary Lou had been over the road to Yorktown Village many times and knew that all she need do was to walk straight on. When she reached the town, she decided, she would ask Mr. Mason, the storekeeper, to tell her how to find the British general. It all seemed a very easy and simple matter to the little girl, as she walked along the pleasant highway that, for some distance, was shaded by tall oaks and growth of locust-trees.

Fortunately for the well-being of Rosecrest in 1781, it was five miles distant from the centre of Yorktown, where Cornwallis was leisurely building fortifications. The British general did not realize that he had walked into a trap that was to end the American Revolution, and give success to the American army. For Lafayette was in camp at Holt's Forge, General Washington's army was marching toward Virginia, and the French fleet was moving toward Chesapeake Bay, at the mouth of York River, to aid the Americans. Cornwallis did not know about Washington or the French fleet; he was still confident that he could take possession of Virginia, and on the very morning when Mary Lou and Lucky started for their walk to Yorktown, Lord Cornwallis had decided that the Americans would not attack his army. If he could have known that Washington was on the march, who can tell how the siege of Yorktown might have ended?

Mary Lou had walked about a mile when Lucky began to be tired, and his whines and frequent stops made the little girl decide to pick him up and carry him for the remainder of the way. But this proved no easy matter, for the small white dog moved about uneasily, and Mary Lou began to wish she had left him at home. She stopped to rest a number of times, for the August sun beat hotly down, and she was tired before she was half-way to her destination.

She was resting in the shade of a wide-spreading beech-tree, when Lucky sprang from her arms and ran into the road barking fiercely, and in a moment two English officers, mounted on fine horses, dashed by. One of them glanced smilingly down at the tiny white dog, whose valiant bark could hardly be heard above the noise of the horses' hoofs, and at the little girl in the muslin dress and flowery hat resting by the wayside.

Mary Lou looked after them wondering if, by any chance, they were bound for Rosecrest, and then, picking up her small companion, she plodded wearily on.

The two horsemen were indeed on their way to Rosecrest. Lord Cornwallis had not forgotten what the cave-man had told him in regard to "a little yellow-haired girl, visiting at Rosecrest, who has a letter addressed to Lord Cornwallis," and, while he did not attach any importance to a letter intrusted to such a messenger, he had mentioned it to one of his officers, saying that if Major Ross wished to ride in the direction of Rosecrest he might obtain the letter. Major Ross promptly agreed, and accompanied by another officer who was disposed for a morning ride, had set forth on this August morning, and reached Rosecrest long before Mary Lou arrived at Yorktown Village.

But she did not enter the town without some difficulties. Cornwallis had already surrounded it with a
line of earthworks, and the astonished little girl found
her way confronted by a line of mounted guns. Armed
soldiers were on guard, and as Mary Lou, holding
Lucky very firmly that he might not bound forward
at the sight of the red-coated soldiers, slowly
advanced, a sharp "Halt!" brought her to a standstill,
and she looked up at a stern-faced guard, who
instantly demanded:

"What do you want? What are you doing here?"

"If you please, I want to see Lieutenant-General Earl
Charles Cornwallis, Commander of the King's Troops,"
Mary Lou responded, recalling the address her Great-
aunt Pamela had written on the letter.

The man's grim face softened at the little girl's care-
ful pronunciation of his general's titles, but he again
questioned her sharply:

"What for? What errand have you with Lord Cornwallis?"

"I have a letter for him; it is in this bag," Mary Lou
said.

The man again regarded her closely. A small girl, not
over nine years old, he decided, could surely not be a
dangerous visitor to admit within the defences of Yorktown, and perhaps she might amuse his lordship, who
seemed a bit dull since there were no British ships in

sight. So, with a brief word of direction, Mary Lou was permitted to pass the guard.

But even then her troubles were not at an end. She hardly knew where she was; the residents had all fled the town when the British entered, and now there were soldiers everywhere. And had not Mary Lou at that moment discovered a familiar figure she might not have been allowed to see the British general. But Lieutenant-Colonel Tarleton was just leaving his headquarters, in the village store, and Mary Lou ran toward him, sure that she had discovered a friend.

The young officer instantly recognized the little girl and smiled down at this unexpected visitor, as he said:

"Well, here is my little cave-girl again! Did you come to do me the honor of a visit?"

Mary Lou quickly told her errand, and Colonel Tarleton listened with evident interest. He walked beside her to Cornwallis's tent, where they were promptly admitted, and Mary Lou, at last, delivered Great-aunt Pamela's letter to Lieutenant-General Earl Charles Cornwallis, Commander of the King's Troops.

CHAPTER XVII

ROSE ELINOR "DRESSES UP"

ROSE ELINOR, from an upper window, had happened to see Mary Lou and Lucky as they went down the garden path, but as both the girls spent a good share of their time in the shady garden walks, Rose Elinor did not for a moment imagine that her small cousin had started for the long walk to Yorktown, and within an hour her thoughts were filled by the arrival of unexpected visitors so that she quite forgot Mary Lou. The two English officers who had passed Mary Lou on the highway reached Rosecrest before Rose Elinor had time to wonder about her cousin's absence.

Rose Elinor happened to be alone in the house, her mother having gone with Mammy Zella and Jasper to the place where they had concealed provisions, when she heard the clatter of horses' hoofs on the driveway, and hoping it might be her father, or perhaps Lafayette himself with Mary Lou's father, she started to run to the front porch, but a glimpse of the scarlet uniforms at once warned her as to who the visitors were.

"Perhaps they have come to warn us to leave Rosecrest," she thought, for she knew that already Cornwallis's officers had taken possession of the Page mansion, and the house of Mr. Nelson. "If Great-aunt Pamela was here I suppose Lord Cornwallis would not let his men trouble the place," thought the little girl, and at the thought she exclaimed, "I could make believe that I was Great-aunt Pamela! She has black eyes, and is little! I could put Mother's lace shawl over my head, and cover myself up on the couch in her room, and make my voice squeak like hers, and scold at them for 'disturbing a loyal old lady.'" And Rose Elinor, in the midst of her fears, giggled at the thought of being able to play a game with the British officers.

But she realized there was no time to lose. In another moment the riders would be at the porch steps. She fled up the stairs to her mother's room, pulled open a bureau drawer and drew out a long scarf of black lace that she twisted about her head, with one corner drooping over her forehead nearly into her eyes. Then, noticing her mother's silver powder-box, she grabbed the powder-puff and hastily whitened her face, so that she was almost startled at the ghastly countenance reflected by the mirror.

Plucky was jumping about the room, barking loudly as he heard the sounds of the stamping horses, the jingle of harness, and at last the steps on the porch, followed by the resounding clang of the big brass knocker.

But Rose Elinor paid no attention to Plucky; she was running about the room drawing the heavy curtains, and when this was done, grasping a bottle of camphor, she curled up on the couch, drew the silken quilt, that lay folded over the back, all about her, so that only a glimpse of a small white face and black eyes could be seen, and with a long breath waited to see what would happen.

Thanks to Plucky she did not have long to wait. The courageous little dog ran to the top of the stairway and with his fiercest barks warned the intruders that they were not to advance another step.

But Major Ross was on the King's business, and as no one responded to his raps and calls, and Plucky's presence at the head of the stairs indicated that whoever was in the house was on the upper floor, he strode up the stairs followed by his companion, and Plucky fled instantly to the darkened chamber and took his place beside his young mistress.

As Major Ross followed the small dog down the hallway he heard a broken voice call: "What is all this noise? Cannot a sick old woman rest in peace?" And the two officers stopped suddenly and looked at each other in amazement.

"Have we, by any chance, entered the wrong house?" whispered the Major, but his companion shook his head and responded:

"This is surely Rosecrest. It is known as the finest estate on the York River. But, apparently, there is no one here excepting some old woman."

"I must find out about that," declared Major Ross, and rapped on the frame of the doorway leading into the shadowy room where Rose Elinor had established herself.

"Who is it?" sounded a squeaky voice. "I declare, I wish I was at Cutting Manor. There's no peace anywhere for loyal Tories."

"'Cutting Manor, loyal Tories,'" repeated Major Scott, and suddenly remembered that Lord Cornwallis had spoken of a visit to an old lady at Cutting Manor.

As he spoke the British officer had advanced, hat in hand, into the shadowy chamber, and bowed to the figure on the couch as he said in a hushed voice:

"I am sorry to disturb you, Madame, but I am sent here by Lord Cornwallis——" Before he could continue the squeaky voice from the huddled figure on the couch interrupted him:

"Earl Charles Cornwallis, Commander of the British forces in Virginia, would never permit his officers to intrude upon Miss Pamela Fairfax Cutting, of Cutting Manor, a loyal subject of the English King."

"Indeed, Miss Cutting, his lordship did not know of your presence at Rosecrest. I am here to secure a letter for his lordship, and if you can tell me where it is, I will at once depart," responded Major Ross. For the ghastly whiteness of the half-hidden face on the couch made him feel sure that the poor old lady must be extremely ill; the broken, squeaky voice convinced him that the excitement of his sudden arrival might be more than anyone evidently so old and feeble could safely withstand, and he was anxious to complete his errand and take his departure.

His companion, who had not spoken, now whispered: "Is the old lady alone here, with no one to look after her?"

Rose Elinor's quick ears heard the question, and she promptly answered it.

"This is the house of my nephew, Mr. Moore. His wife and servants are somewhere in the grounds. Please say to Earl Cornwallis that I expect to stay here ———" At this point the squeaky voice seemed to die away in a sudden faintness, and Major Ross started forward thinking the old lady might need prompt assistance, but the camphor bottle appeared, and its stinging odor filled the chamber so that both the officers choked and sneezed, and the old lady seemed greatly revived as she continued in a stronger tone: "And I must not be disturbed by soldiers. I expect this place to be protected," and now the old lady coughed and choked, while Plucky ran under the couch in a vain endeavor to escape the fumes of camphor that now filled the room.

"I am sure his lordship will give this place every protection while you remain here," declared Major Ross. "And now I must get the letter and return to camp."

"Tell the Earl I know all about the letter, and it is of no importance," responded the squeaky voice.

"I am quite ready to accept the word of Miss Pamela Fairfax Cutting, and I will deliver your message to his lordship. Can we not call your cousin, or a servant, to assist you?" asked the officer, for "the old lady" seemed to be in danger of choking, and Major Ross was becoming rather alarmed.

"No indeed!" came the muffled response. "Must be quiet; can't stand noise."

The two officers both nodded at this, and, as the old lady had drawn the silk quilt up so that only her eyes could be seen, they both bowed low to "the loyal old Tory," as they afterward described her, and tiptoed from the room and down the stairs. But before they reached the lower hall Mammy Zella appeared on the porch. She had seen the horses on the driveway, and believing that her master and Mr. Abbott had arrived, had hurried toward the house. Now, seeing the two redcoats tiptoeing so carefully down the stairs, she was instantly convinced that a party of raiders had come to strip the house. But Mammy Zella had a valiant spirit; raiders or not, these redcoats should not escape without hearing her opinion of such actions, and she took her place at the foot of the stairs and demanded to know: "Wha' for yo'uns a-skulkin' 'bout dis house fer?"

For a second Major Ross was too surprised at so unaccustomed a salutation to make any reply, then, with a scowling glance, he said quickly:

"You had better attend to poor old Miss Cutting, and not leave the old lady alone in that dark chamber," adding, as he strode past the astonished darkey: "Tell Mrs. Moore that she and her family need have no alarm. As long as Miss Cutting remains here, Rosecrest will not be harmed; nor will she again be intruded upon."

"Fo' de lan' sakes," muttered Mammy Zella, staring after the two British officers as they mounted their fine horses and rode swiftly down the driveway. "I reckon dey's los' der reason. How cum dey 'magine ole Miss Cuttin' h'ar? But if dey *be* gone crazy, mebbe 'tis a good t'ing, an' I'll sure tell Mistus Moore wot dey say," and Mammy Zella started off to the kitchen to tell Mrs. Moore of the "crazy" British officers, and of their promise that Rosecrest should be protected.

The moment Major Ross and his companion had left the shadowy room Rose Elinor sprang off the couch, drew back the curtains from the windows, and hurriedly untwisted the black lace scarf from about her head; then, seizing a towel, she endeavored to remove the heavy coating of powder. In opening the camphor-bottle she had spilled its entire contents, and when Mrs. Moore entered the chamber she was a little startled at the disorder of the room, and at the strong odor of camphor.

"What has happened?" she questioned anxiously, as Rose Elinor ran past her toward the hallway.

"I dressed up, and spilled the camphor," Rose Elinor called back, eager to find Mary Lou and describe what fun it had been to fool the fine British officers, and win the promise that Rosecrest should be protected.

Mrs. Moore picked up the lace scarf, straightened the couch cushions and folded the quilt. The two little cousins often "dressed up" in her gowns; but Mary Lou always put everything carefully back in its proper place; so now Mrs. Moore wondered a little that her small cousin had left the chamber in disorder, for she took it for granted that Mary Lou had been with Rose Elinor. Mammy Zella's excited account of her encounter with the British officers gave Mrs. Moore the hope that the soldiers would not again trouble the family at Rosecrest. "And all because we are Aunt Pamela's relatives," she decided, with a kindly thought for the rigid old Tory, who was now sailing toward her beloved England.

Rose Elinor ran down the porch steps calling her cousin's name; but it was Mammy Zella who responded.

"Yo' tumble in de flour? Wot yo' bin a-doin' of?" demanded the old colored woman, her sharp eyes fixed on the powdery streaks that still lingered on Rose Elinor's face.

"Oh, Mammy! Mammy! I've been having fun. I dressed up, and put powder on my face!" laughed the little girl, as she danced about on the porch step, wishing that everybody could know of how cleverly she had fooled two English officers, yet not daring to tell the story to anyone excepting to Mary Lou.

"I 'clar ter goodness! Dis ain' no time fer sich actions," responded Mammy disapprovingly. But her young mistress laughed delightedly, and declared:

"Oh! Yes, it is; just the time, Mammy," and again calling her cousin's name, Rose Elinor ran down between the tall rose-bushes, with Plucky close behind her.

While Rose Elinor had been so skilfully impersonating Great-aunt Pamela, Mary Lou and Lucky had reached Yorktown and had been introduced to Governor Cornwallis.

The famous English general had received her kindly, and after opening and reading Miss Cutting's letter, he had questioned the little girl as to the family at Rosecrest. Mary Lou told him that there was no one there excepting Rose Elinor, Mrs. Moore, and the two servants, and added quickly: "And, if you please, Lieutenant-General Earl Charles Cornwallis, Commander of the King's Troops, they do not know I have brought you Great-aunt Pamela's letter." And then, as the friendly general seemed interested, Mary Lou eagerly told him her own sad little story, and of all the kindness she had received at Rosecrest.

"And so I wanted to do something for them. And, if you please, Lieutenant-General Earl Charles Cornwallis, don't let anybody hurt them or drive them away from Rosecrest," and the little girl looked up with pleading eyes into the face of the man who then believed he would soon conquer Virginia.

It seemed a very small favor to grant this girl's request, and at the same time oblige so loyal a subject of King George the Third as Miss Pamela Fairfax Cutting, and Mary Lou was told that no harm should come to Rosecrest through the troops encamped at Yorktown.

The little girl thanked Lord Cornwallis, curtseyed, and with Lucky in her arms started to leave the tent, when she suddenly stopped short. "Lovely," she whispered, staring at a doll with a battered face, with one arm missing, and clothed only in shreds of torn muslin, and suspended by a string tied about its neck, from a cord that ran across one corner of the tent.

"What's that?" questioned Cornwallis, leaving his seat and standing beside his little visitor.

"That's my doll! The cave-man grabbed her and threw her away. Her name is 'Lovely,'" said Mary Lou soberly. "What is she hung up there for?"

Lord Cornwallis made no answer; stepping toward the swaying, broken doll he loosened the cord about its neck and in a moment Mary Lou had set Lucky down, and again held her beloved "Lovely." There was little resemblance to the "Lovely" of last May, but Mary Lou's affection remained unchanged. "I can mend her," she gravely assured her companion, and again bade him good-bye. She stepped from the tent, to find Colonel Tarleton waiting for her.

"I am riding toward Rosecrest and will take you along," he said, then noticing the battered doll, he added: "I brought that from the cave on Gloucester Point yesterday."

"Oh, thank you! She's my doll! And you saved her just as you did me," said Mary Lou eagerly.

Tarleton's face flushed. For poor "Lovely" had been labeled "Washington," and had been "hung as a traitor to King George," for the amusement of Lord Cornwallis.

Tarleton set Mary Lou down only a short distance from the entrance to Rosecrest, and she came slowly up the path, followed by the discouraged Lucky, just as Mrs. Moore began to fear that some harm might have befallen her.

CHAPTER XVIII

EXPLANATIONS

MARY LOU listened with wondering eyes as Rose Elinor laughingly described the English officer's anxiety over Great-aunt Pamela's condition.

Mary Lou thought that no one excepting her wonderful cousin could have been clever enough to think of such a plan, and, at the same time, realized that her long walks in the hot August sun to deliver the letter to Earl Cornwallis had been a useless endeavor. "But if I had not gone I would not have found 'Lovely,'" she exclaimed, and forgetting her intention not to let anyone see her beloved doll until she had made some effort to restore her, she held out the battered doll for Rose Elinor to see.

For an instant Rose Elinor was too surprised to speak; then she exclaimed: "Have you seen the cave-man?"

Mary Lou shook her head, and a little smile crept over her face.

"No! I went to Yorktown to give Great-aunt Pamela's letter to Earl Charles Cornwallis, Lieutenant-General of the King's forces, and the kind officer who saved us from the cave-man had saved 'Lovely,' too, and gave her back to me," and Mary Lou's gaze again rested lovingly on poor "Lovely."

Rose Elinor's eyes closed as tightly as if a spring had been touched, and her surprised cousin heard the whispered "One—and—Two—and Three."

But this time even the "witch's charm" did not seem effective; for a moment later Rose Elinor, without another word to her cousin, ran toward the house.

Mary Lou, puzzled and unhappy, slowly followed her.

All the little girl's joy in having at last, as she thought, been of some service to the cousins who had so befriended her, was clouded and spoiled. For the moment she even forgot "Lovely."

"I guess it would have been better if I had not carried the letter," she thought unhappily, sitting down on the lower step of the porch. "Rose Elinor is angry at me, and I didn't do any good, and I am tired."

It was half an hour later when Mammy Zella, coming around the house, discovered the little girl, holding what remained of the cherished "Lovely," fast asleep on the porch step. Lucky was curled up beside her, and Mammy was quick to notice that the little dog, as well as his small mistress, was dusty and evidently tired.

"Dey's bin up ter sum' contrapshuns," she promptly decided. "An' so has Rose Elinor, wid her face all flour!"

Very gently Mammy Zella awakened the little girl. "Yo' dinnah's a-waitin', an' dar is sum fine hot 'lasses cake! Wot yo' t'ink ob dat?" and Mammy smiled down at the woebegone little face.

"An' my lan'! Ef yo' ain' foun' yo' doll! Now, dat am good luck! Jes' as soon as yo' eats yo' dinnah, we'll men' her all fine!" she continued.

"Can you mend her, Mammy? Oh! Can you?" questioned Mary Lou, forgetting all her troubles in so splendid a possibility as having "Lovely" restored to some degree of her former beauty.

"Sho' I can!" declared Mammy. "Yo' step 'long to de dinin' room, an' bimeby yo' an' I'll fix de doll all gran'!"

And so convincing was Mammy's voice and manner that Mary Lou ran in to luncheon, thinking only of her doll, and sure that "Lovely" would be restored to beauty.

But at Mrs. Moore's question as to where Mary Lou had been during the long forenoon the little girl's face clouded. But she did not hesitate for a moment.

"I went to Yorktown to carry Great-aunt Pamela's letter to Earl Charles Cornwallis, Lieutenant-General of the King's forces," she replied soberly. And, as Mrs. Moore listened in astonishment, Mary Lou told the story of her effort to secure protection for Rosecrest, and of Colonel Tarleton having brought the doll from the cave at Gloucester Point.

"And did General Cornwallis promise you that we should not be molested?" Mrs. Moore asked anxiously; for she was sadly worried by the nearness of the invaders.

"Yes, indeed! But if I had not taken Great-aunt Pamela's letter it would have been just the same, for Rose Elinor made believe—"

"Tell-tale! Tell-tale!" sounded an angry voice, and Mary Lou stopped suddenly as Rose Elinor flung herself into the dining-room, and standing facing her little cousin, began speaking so rapidly that it was evident the "witch's charm" had not availed this time, and that she could not control her temper.

"Yes, I did 'make believe,' but I did not mean to tell my mother about it until I got ready," and she poured forth the entire story of her clever plan for deceiving the British officers.

"And Mary Lou has done a dreadful thing in taking that letter to the English general! It was a letter from Lafayette!" she concluded.

Long before Rose Elinor reached this point in her story poor Mary Lou's head had begun to droop, and now it rested on the table as she choked back her sobs.

"From Lafayette? Rose Elinor! What do you mean?" questioned her mother.

"He gave it to me! I took Great-aunt Pamela's old Tory letter out of Mary Lou's trunk, the day you went to Colonel Carter's. I rode Sooty to Lafayette's camp. And I gave him the letter, and he wrote another and I brought it home and put it in Mary Lou's trunk. And that is the letter she carried to the British general!"

Rose Elinor concluded triumphantly, with a scornful glance toward the yellow head of her cousin.

Rose Elinor had been confident that she had performed a very brave and loyal deed in delivering a "Tory" letter to the French general. She had expected that, when her mother discovered it, she would be praised and told that she deserved a reward. Therefore she was greatly astonished to see her mother's severe expression, and to hear her say:

"Rose Elinor Moore. Do you mean to tell me that, without Mary Lou's knowledge, you took a letter from her trunk, and delivered it to a person for whom it was not intended?"

Rose Elinor nodded, her surprised glance fixed upon her mother's face, and the angry crimson fading from her cheeks.

"And do you for one moment suppose that General Lafayette would open a letter from Aunt Pamela Fairfax?" she questioned, "especially when the inscription proved that it was a plea to protect a harmless child? General Lafayette gave you back unopened the letter you carried to him. He simply enclosed it in another wrapper in order not to hurt your feelings. I am as sure of that as if he had told me. He saw that you were an unthinking little girl, and I hope he understood that you did not realize your dishonorable action. All you can do now is to tell your cousin you are sorry, and ask her to pardon you."

Never before had Rose Elinor been so sternly disapproved by her indulgent mother; never before had she been asked to own herself in the wrong, and now all her joy in the thought of having been of service to America; all her delight in the trick she had so cleverly played on the British officers that morning, was swept away as she stood pale and abashed under her mother's disapproval, and when Mrs. Moore turned to Mary Lou saying:

"You were indeed brave, dear child, to carry the letter to Cornwallis. I know you did it hoping to help us all and to protect Rosecrest, and I will always remember it," and, without another word to Rose Elinor, she led Mary Lou from the room. Rose began to cry quietly.

"I wanted to protect Rosecrest," Rose Elinor whispered unhappily. She did not want any luncheon; she could think only of her mother's words: that she, Rose Elinor Moore, a young lady of Virginia, had acted dishonorably in taking the letter to Lafayette.

"If Great-aunt Pamela wasn't a Tory it never would have happened," she thought, in her endeavor to reassure herself. Then she remembered her mother had said that all she could do was to ask Mary Lou's pardon and to say she was sorry.

"Well," she said aloud, with a long sigh, "I can do that. It's what I've been doing ever since Mary Lou came to Rosecrest," and she followed her mother and Mary Lou to the platform on the roof.

"Please forgive me, Mary Lou. I'm sorry," she said simply, and in a moment Mary Lou's arms were close about her, and she heard her mother say, "Darling child."

After all, she thought, perhaps she would like some luncheon, and hand-in-hand the two cousins returned to the dining-room, and devoured the " 'lasses cake," Mary Lou urging her cousin to again describe how she had dropped the camphor-bottle, and made her voice "squeaky."

"I think it was splendid!" Mary Lou declared earnestly; "and your mother said it must have been funny enough, to see the fine British officers apologizing for disturbing you. She said it would make Governor Jefferson laugh Bell when he heard it!"

"Oh! Did she indeed say that? I am so glad you told me," Rose Elinor responded eagerly. "Do you think Lafayette believed me dishonorable to bring him the letter, Mary Lou?" she asked soberly.

Mary Lou shook her head as she answered: "Of course he did not. He knew you wanted to help him defeat Cornwallis; that's what he thought."

And that was exactly what the French general did think, and he often recalled Rose Elinor's visit, her ride through woodland paths and across fields, to bring him a letter that she hoped would give him valuable information. When he thus remembered her it was as a brave little maid of Virginia.

When the last crumb of "'lasses" cake had been devoured, the cousins cleared off the table, carrying the dishes to the kitchen for Mammy Zella to wash. They were both tired from the excitements and unexpected happenings of the day, and quite ready to accept Mrs. Moore's suggestion to go to their own room for a nap.

While the little girls slept Mammy Zella busied herself in the endeavor to repair the abused doll. First of all, she cut from a bit of stout cloth a shape resembling "Lovely"'s remaining arm, and stuffed it with cotton, shaping tiny fingers, and stitching them with great care. This arm she fastened securely to the doll's shoulder. Poor "Lovely"'s face puzzled Mammy.

"De nose am gone, and de cheeks bruk," she murmured dolefully. "I reckon Mistus Moore bettah jes' tek a luk at dis face," and she promptly went in search of her mistress, and told her of Mary Lou's affection for "Lovely."

"Jes' seems if dat chile coul'n' stan' gibbin' up dis ole doll," Mammy explained. "But luk at dis face!" and she held out the disfigured doll.

"I believe we can mend her face, Mammy," Mrs. Moore replied hopefully. "Bring me the ball of wax from my work-basket."

Mammy hastened to obey, and then followed her mistress to the kitchen, and watched with admiring eyes while Mrs. Moore put the wax to melt over the bed of hot ashes; then carefully turned the wax over "Lovely"'s broken face, and, as it began to harden, molded a new nose, and filled and smoothed the cracked cheeks.

"Ef dat ain' mos' a mirrikil," muttered the delighted Mammy. And when the wax had completely hardened and she watched her mistress take a tiny brush from Rose Elinor's box of water-color paints and delicately tint "Lovely"'s face with pink, restored the scarlet of her lips, and the brown of her hair, Mammy chuckled with satisfaction.

"Dat am jes' splendiferous. I 'clar it be. Now, if dar be a dress fur dis doll, Miss Ma'y Lou gwine ter belibe sum angel bin a dealin' wid her," declared Mammy.

There were plenty of clothes for "Lovely," and she was soon dressed in the very best of flounces and embroidered petticoats, muslin dress, and silken sash of pale pink; a cape of white broadcloth and a tiny hat of white silk added to the elegance of her toilette, and when late that afternoon Mary Lou awoke and found this smiling, well-dressed doll sitting at the foot of her bed, she stared in amazement.

But Mammy was peering in from the open doorway.

"Wot I tell yo', Miss Ma'y Lou? Wot I tell yo'? Ain' dat doll jes' as fine as she ebber was? Ain' she?" she chuckled, and, with a little gasp of surprise, Mary Lou whispered: "'Lovely'!"

CHAPTER XIX

NEWS FROM YORKTOWN

EARLY in September the household at Rosecrest were surprised by a visit from its master, accompanied by Mary Lou's father. They arrived in the early hours of one evening and remained until the darkness of the following night.

The story of Rose Elinor's "make believe," that had so deceived the English officers, delighted her father, and he also declared, as Mrs. Moore had done, that Mr. Jefferson must hear it, and both Mary Lou and Rose Elinor were praised for their endeavor to protect Rosecrest from the invading army. Mr. Moore, with a number of other Virginia gentlemen who were not able to be soldiers, were now, under Mr. Jefferson's direction, securing supplies from the neighboring countryside for the American troops, and Mrs. Moore and the little girls listened eagerly as he told them of the French fleet, under De Grasse, that was now just out side Chesapeake Bay, ready to aid in the capture of the British troops when General Washington should decide that the moment for attack had arrived.

"It is a noble fleet," Mr. Moore declared; "twenty-eight sail-of-the-line and six frigates, and the flagship *Ville de Paris*, that carries one hundred and twenty guns, and is the grandest ship afloat on all the seas."

"It only remains now for Washington's troops to reach Lafayette's force, and the march upon Cornwallis will begin," said Captain Abbott.

Mr. Moore felt that Aunt Pamela had done them all a great service in writing the letter to Cornwallis, and told of his visit to Cutting Manor and the discovery that Miss Pamela Fairfax Cutting had sailed for England.

Mary Lou became a little sober at this news; it meant that she might never again see the stern old lady, whose thought for the protection of her small niece had perhaps saved Rosecrest from being occupied by English soldiers.

"I shall never forget Great-aunt Pamela," she said slowly, and her father quickly responded:

"We have great reason to love and remember her, my dear. And perhaps next year she may decide to return to Virginia, and then you can tell her of our gratitude."

Mr. Moore declared that the siege of Yorktown would prove the great surprise of the American Revolution. "A glorious end of these years of conflict," he said, smiling down at his little daughter.

The next two weeks passed quietly with the household at Rosecrest. Every morning the little cousins hurried to the platform on the roof, to gaze off toward that glimpse of the road leading from Williamsburg to York-town, down which Washington's army would advance. And early on the morning of September 28, 1781, Mary Lou, who had been the first to reach the platform, saw the blue of the uniforms of the French and Continental soldiers as they marched leisurely on to the scene of their coming triumph.

Mary Lou's calls quickly brought Rose Elinor and Mrs. Moore, followed by Mammy Zella and Jasper, to the housetop, and the little group silently watched the distant line of marching men as they moved steadily forward under the clear September sky.

By early afternoon the American army lay around Yorktown in the shape of a new moon. In this way York-town was regularly invested from the land side, while the French fleet watched on the water, ready to meet any British ships that attempted to approach.

That noon when Mammy Zella called Jasper to eat his dinner, he did not appear, and it was early night-fall when he slunk into the kitchen, saying:

"I jes' 'bliged ter fin' out w'at was a-doin' 'tween de armies. An' fur as I kin see, dar ain' nuffin' doin'. I reck-on dat British generil am a-waitin' fer mo' sogers to 'rive. De 'Merican army an' de British army are 'bout a mile apart. An' I'll bet de Britishers 'll jes' kinder step back a little ways ter-night."

And Jasper was right. During the night the British retired within the immediate defences of

Yorktown. But this step was of small importance. There were skirmishes between the armies, and both English and American soldiers were not lacking in valor.

The siege had begun. English ships had entered Chesapeake Bay. One of these was named the *Charon*, and the other the *Guadaloupe*, and as they sailed up the York River they were fired upon with red-hot cannonballs from the American redoubts, and both the ships were soon set on fire. From the roof of Rosecrest the little girls saw this wild and terrible spectacle, as the flames caught the sails and rigging of the ships and ran to the tops of the masts.

Day after day the fighting continued. Mrs. Moore's anxiety increased with every hour, and she often said that she longed for news as to the Americans' success. Mary Lou and Rose Elinor also earnestly wished they could know if their fathers were with Washington and Lafayette. They talked of nothing but the battle that was so near them; and when Rose Elinor whispered to her cousin that she had a plan by which they could safely discover if the American troops were winning, Mary Lou was quite ready to listen.

"I'll make believe be Great-aunt Pamela again," said Rose Elinor.

"I can wear an old black dress that hangs in Mother's closet, and an old bonnet and veil, and go straight to Yorktown."

"You can't, Rose Elinor! They have rows of guns, and besides that, the Americans wouldn't let you," Mary Lou responded soberly.

"Yes, they would. We'd go in the pony-cart; I'd say you were my great-niece; we'd manage And we could find out if Americans were winning."

Mary Lou was always quite ready to believe that her wonderful cousin could do whatever she pleased to do, and now agreed to the plan. Both the girls realized that it must be kept a secret.

"When we come home and can tell Mother just which any will win, and perhaps have splendid news, why, she will think it is all right," said Rose Elinor confidently.

The old black dress, bonnet and veil, and Mrs. Moore's box of powder were carried carefully away to a hiding-place near the road, and early on the morning they had chosen for their journey, Rose Elinor and Mary Lou dragged the pony-cart from the carriage house down a back road to the highway. It proved a more difficult matter to catch the ponies, who were in an open field, but they finally succeeded, and led Blacky and Sooty to the highway, where they managed to harness them to the cart, and, fastening the surprised ponies to a near-by tree, the girls hastened back to the house in time for breakfast.

As soon as breakfast was over the girls sauntered into the garden, commanding Lucky and Plucky to remain in the house. Once out of sight of the porch they fled toward the highway; and in a short time the black ponies were trotting swiftly along the road to Yorktown, driven by an old lady who, had there been anyone to observe her, would have seemed in unusually gay spirits for so venerable an appearing person.

It was the morning of October 17, 1781, the morning chosen by Cornwallis for his surrender. The brilliant feats of the American soldiers, and his own failure to make an attempted escape, had left him no other course; and as Rose Elinor and Mary Lou drove along the highway to Yorktown, a British drummer in red had mounted a parapet at Yorktown and began to beat a "parley." With this drummer appeared an officer waving a white handkerchief, the "flag of truce." He was met and blindfolded by an American officer, and conducted to the rear of the American lines. It was the end of British domination in America.

A sudden hush had fallen upon the countryside. For days the volleying of guns along the banks of the York River had become a familiar sound to the little cousins; and now as the reports ceased, as only the bird-calls, and the rustle of the autumn leaves broke the stillness, they looked at each other in surprise.

"P'raps the war is over!" suggested Mary Lou hopefully.

"I don't believe wars end so quietly," Rose Elinor responded thoughtfully, and, with a quick exclamation of surprise, she brought the ponies to a standstill; for coming down the highway, at a swinging gallop, were two American soldiers.

They drew rein as they neared the pony-team and called out: "Turn about; this road is closed."

"What for? I wish to go to Yorktown," Rose Elinor called back.

"Cornwallis has given up. He has this hour asked a parley," replied the excited man. "By to-morrow he will be Washington's prisoner."

"Hurrah!" shouted his companion waving a shabby cap, and then, apparently noticing that one of the passengers in the pony-cart was an elderly lady, he added: "Turn your ponies, Madam, and return home. A guard will stop you if you go further on."

But Rose Elinor was already turning Blacky and Sooty toward home. "'Cornwallis has given up. By to-morrow he will be Washington's prisoner,'" she repeated, and urged the ponies to a constantly faster pace, until the little cart swayed and bounced over the rough road; and, as the team dashed up the driveway, and Mrs. Moore, surprised and alarmed, appeared on the steps of the porch, the little girls both shouted the good news, "Cornwallis has given up."

In the delight and excitement that followed this announcement, Mrs. Moore hardly noticed Rose Elinor's strange costume, and not until the little girl stumbled over the long black skirt and fell flat on the upper step of the porch, did Mammy Zella, with her usual good-natured chuckle, pointing at the queer little figure, say:

"Jes' look dar, Missus. Ef dat ain' de span image ob Missus Pamela, w'at useter visit us."

Even then Mrs. Moore asked no questions. She realized all it meant, not only to Rosecrest, but to all the world, that Lord Cornwallis, one of the most estimable men of England, and considered their best general, should surrender to Washington's army, and she paid no further attention to the little girls that morning. Rose Elinor pulled off the black dress and bonnet that Mammy promptly took charge of, and she and Mary Lou hastened to the roof, hoping to see something on highway or river that might tell them more of the great affairs then taking place so near to Rosecrest.

There was nothing to be seen or heard, but, quiet and peaceful as it seemed, neither of the girls cared for their usual games. They talked of Lafayette; of Colonel Tarleton, and of the cave where the English officer had found Mary Lou. And when Mr. Moore reached home that afternoon and confirmed the good news of Cornwallis's surrender, Mary Lou clasped her restored "Lovely," with a grateful thought for the daring English officer who was now a prisoner of war.

Mr. Moore said it would not be possible for Mary Lou's father to arrive at Rosecrest until after the formal ceremony of the surrender of the British troops to Washington.

"That will surely take place on the nineteenth, day after to-morrow," said Mr. Moore. "And it will be a spectacle that you will both remember all your lives."

"Oh, Father! Are we to see it?" exclaimed Rose Elinor; while Mary Lou's blue eyes opened more widely than ever at such a possibility.

"Certainly, you are to see it," Mr. Moore replied.

CHAPTER XX

"CLEOPATRA"

EARLY on the morning of October 19, 1781, Blacky and Sooty, whose black coats shone, and whose harnesses had been polished until they caught every ray of sunlight, were harnessed to the pony-cart, and Rose Elinor and Mary Lou, wearing their best dresses, and the hats that Mrs. Moore had hastily trimmed with the American colors of red, white and blue, took their places in the cart, and followed the carriage containing Mr. and Mrs. Moore, Mammy Zella and Jasper, down the driveway on their way to Yorktown, to view the ceremony of Cornwallis's surrender.

Mr. Moore had borrowed the carriage and horses, as his own were still in possession of the British. As they drove along the highway Mr. Moore now and then exchanged salutations with friends who, like himself, were on their way to witness the crowning act of the success of the American Revolution.

Securing a position on a slope not far from the Hampton Road, after having left the carriage and pony-cart at a nearby house, the little party from Rosecrest gazed down upon the English troops as they marched out from Yorktown, and surrendered their arms to the victorious Americans.

The French and American armies were drawn up on either side of the way, the French troops presenting a brilliant spectacle in their white uniforms, with plumed and decorated officers at their head, and their silken flags floating along the line. The American troops, war-worn and shabby, showing their privations and hardships, bore themselves nobly.

At the head of the lines were their generals, superbly mounted: Washington, Lafayette, Rochambeau, Lincoln, Steuben and Knox, and others.

"There's Lafayette!" Rose Elinor whispered in a voice hushed by awe, and wondered that she had ever dared venture into his presence, and her face flushed a little, as she recalled the errand on which she had gone.

Leading the British came General O'Hara instead of Cornwallis, as the latter had pleaded illness, sending his sword by O'Hara to be given up to Washington, as a token of the enemy's submission. And among the English officers, Rose Elinor was quick to recognize the two who had been received at Rosecrest by "Great-aunt Pamela," and she eagerly pointed them out to Mary Lou; whose own glance was fixed admiringly upon the handsome Tarleton, with perhaps the only friendly look the young English officer ever received from an American.

The ceremony that the little girls remembered all their lives, and that they described to their grandchildren when they were old ladies, was soon over. The British troops marched between the two lines of their conquerors, and stacked their arms and colors, and then returned to their quarters as prisoners of war. The Revolutionary War was at an end.

Captain Abbott drove home with the Moores, and that night a huge bonfire on the hill back of Rosecrest flashed an answer to fires on many another Virginia hilltop in rejoicing that the invading army was conquered. And when, a few weeks later, Mr. Thomas Jefferson was again Rosecrest's honored guest, he laughed heartily over the story of "Great-aunt Pamela" and the English officers, and heard also of Mary Lou's visit to the English camp.

As Mr. Jefferson said good-bye to the little girls, he smiled down at Mary Lou and said:

"And so my little Tory maid proved to be a loyal American after all."

Mary Lou made her best curtsey as she responded:

"If you please, sir, 'twas you cured me of being a Tory.

"Down with all Tories! Hurrah for Lafayette," sounded a gruff voice from the hallway, as "Cleopatra" ruffled her feathers and peered out at the happy group on the porch steps at Rosecrest.

190   *A LITTLE MAID*

The Stories in This Series Are: